Teachers' Notes for
BEAM's Big Book of

Word

Problems

for Years 1 and 2

Mike Askew

BEAM Education

BEAM Education is a specialist mathematics education publisher, dedicated to promoting the teaching and learning of mathematics as interesting, challenging and enjoyable. Their materials cover teaching and learning needs from the age of 3 to 14 and they offer consultancy and training.
BEAM is an acknowledged expert in the field of mathematics education.

Published by BEAM Education
Maze Workshops
72a Southgate Road
London N1 3JT
info@beam.co.uk

Orders:
orderline 01242 267945
beamorders@nelsonthornes.com

www.beam.co.uk

© BEAM Education 2005
All rights reserved. None of the material in the Big Book may be reproduced or published in any form without prior permission from the publisher. The photocopiable worksheets in the Teachers' Notes may be reproduced by individual schools without permission from the publisher. No other material in the Teachers' Notes may be reproduced or published in any form without prior permission from the publisher. The CD-ROM may be used by individual schools as summarised in the Teachers' Notes.

Big Book and Teachers' Notes text © Mike Askew
The author's moral rights have been asserted.

ISBN 1 903142 48 2
British Library Cataloguing-in-Publication Data
Data available

Edited by Raewyn Glynn
Designed by Malena Wilson-Max

Big Book illustrations by John Bendall-Brunello, Jo Brown and Jan McCafferty
© John Bendall-Brunello
(Big Book pp 1, 4, 6, 11, 12, 19, 20, 23)
© Jo Brown
(Big Book pp 2, 3, 5, 7, 9, 15, 21, 24)
© Jan McCafferty
(Big Book pp 8, 10, 13, 14, 16, 17, 18, 22)

Printed in the UK by Cromwell Press Ltd

Introduction	*5*
Objectives	*11*
The 24 Units	*13*
Year 1	*14*
Year 2	*38*
Unit problem sheets	*63*
[photocopiables]	
Year 1	*64*
Year 2	*88*

This Word Problems resource comprises the Big Book, for use with children in Years 1 and 2, the Teachers' Notes (with photocopiable worksheets) and a CD-ROM.

The 24 units in this resource provide a way of helping children move from being novice problem solvers to being expert problem solvers. Research has shown that there are some key differences between novice and expert problem solvers.

- **Novice problem solvers** look at the various parts of a problem and try to put them together to make sense of the problem.

- **Expert problem solvers** get an overall feel for what the problem is about and then seek out the parts that will help in a solution.

- **Novice problem solvers** treat each problem in isolation from other problems that they have worked on: they try to figure out what the problem is about simply by looking at the information given.

- **Expert problem solvers** treat each problem as being one of a generic class of problems: they ask themselves 'have I seen anything like this before?'

An example illustrates this. Consider the calculation 38 ÷ 6. Before reading on, try to think of a real world situation where the sensible answer to 38 ÷ 6 means rounding up the mathematical answer of 6 remainder 2 to 7.

Were you thinking of putting 38 eggs into egg boxes, or possibly people into mini-buses or tents? If not, your example is still probably not too far away from these. This is no mind-reading trick; many people choose problems of this sort for division situations where you need to round up.

These 24 units work on helping children begin to build up their knowledge of 'classes of problems' and the language to describe them. So when they meet a new problem they, like expert problem solvers, can think about what else they have seen that is similar and use appropriate language to describe the type of problem.

This approach is different from one that encourages strategies like looking for 'keywords'. The keywords approach rests on the assumption that the meaning of a problem somehow lies within the wording of the problem itself. The expert/novice approach works on the assumption that the problem solver has to bring meaning to the wording of the problem. This is similar to research into reading and the idea that expert readers have mental 'frames' that they draw on in order to make sense of text. Consider, for example:

Sheila and Mike were excited as they finished decorating John's cake.
They wondered if he would manage to blow out all the candles in one go.

The expert reader has no difficulty knowing that this is about preparing for a birthday party. But there is no mention of birthdays or parties: they bring that meaning to the words through the mental 'frame' they have for birthday parties.

Sheila and Mike each started to make sandwiches.
Sheila made 20 sandwiches and Mike made 5.
How many more sandwiches did Sheila make than Mike?

The expert problem solver recognises this as a one of the class of problems from their frame of 'subtraction as difference' (comparing two separate groups). In other words, they use analogical reasoning. The novice might concentrate on the wording in the problem rather than the meaning they bring to it, and are likely to add, based on the word 'more'. Or they may divide, since the word 'each' is there and 5 divides into 20 rather nicely. Such 'deductive' reasoning based on 'clues' in the words and numbers is less helpful.

These lessons help children develop the analogical reasoning used by the expert problem solver. Expert problem solvers do use deductive thinking as well, and we need to encourage children in this way of thinking. But we also need to acknowledge the power of analogical thinking.

Teaching a Word Problem lesson

The 24 units are evenly split between Year 1 and Year 2. The first twelve units are designed for the younger age group, but you can use this structure flexibly.

Some children in Year 1 will be able to go on to some of the Year 2 problems. Equally, some children in Year 2 may benefit from looking at the Year 1 problems.

You can integrate the 24 lessons with other lessons in one of two ways. Firstly, you could teach the Word Problem lessons following a regular pattern (once a fortnight, for example). The advantage of this is that the contents of each lesson have two weeks to 'simmer' in children's minds, so steady consolidation of the ideas takes place. Secondly, you could select specific Word Problem lessons and teach them alongside other lessons that deal with similar types of calculation.

The objectives chart on page 11 will help you integrate the Word Problem lessons with other plans; the chart indicates the type of calculation covered by each problem.

Each Word Problem lesson in this resource takes the same basic form. This is so that children get used to what is expected of them in the lesson and they can then concentrate on thinking about the mathematics.

There are four parts to the lesson:

- solving the Big Book problems
- linking up the problems
- follow-up problems
- wrap-up.

Introduction

Solving the Big Book problems

Each page of the Big Book has two word problems on it. Preferably working in pairs, the children solve each of the problems in turn. Before moving on to the next problem there is a whole class discussion about the ways in which they interpreted the problem and the strategies used for solving it. The emphasis here is on direct teaching, not teaching directively. In other words, the role of the teacher is to support the children in their struggle to make sense of the problems rather than to explicitly direct them to use particular methods. When discussing the ways in which the children set about solving the problems, the role of the teacher is to support the children's explanations through asking clarifying questions, setting up models, pictures or diagrams, and to introduce notation that helps the other children understand a child's approach.

The pages in the Teachers' Notes provide specific suggestions for the sort of children's methods to look out for and ways to support the development of these.

Linking up the problems

In the second phase of the whole class introduction, the emphasis shifts from thinking about each problem separately to looking at the set of three and considering ways in which they are linked. On the Big Book pages, the two problems have been chosen to be representative of a class of problems.

The second part of the whole class introduction is designed to draw children's attention to the common mathematical structure underlying the problems. This is supported by giving labels to classes of problems and using the imagery of the situations to help children build up their own images for groups of problems.

Once again, the Teachers' Notes provide explicit guidance on what to focus the children's attention on.

Follow-up problems

After the initial whole class discussion of the Big Book problems and the links between them, the children then have time to work more independently on the ideas that have been introduced.

Children work individually on follow-up problem sheets (given as photocopiables) that consolidate and develop the ideas introduced in the whole class part of the lesson. The problem sheets are provided here at two levels of difficulty (A and B). The basic mathematical structure of the word problem is the same on both sheets so that all children can focus on this aspect. The problems on sheet A are very similar to those in the Big Book, while the ones on Sheet B are more open-ended and allow the children to have some control over the level of numerical difficulty.

If you think the children are mature enough, encourage them to join up with a partner and share their work. During this sharing, individuals are allowed to change their working and answers, but in ways that still preserve their own, original and independent working. Using a different coloured pen or pencil could help them make clear the distinction between their first workings and their workings with a partner. Erasers are definitely banned!

Wrap-up

Finally, the whole class comes back together again to further explore the nature of the problems and reinforce the key underlying ideas.

Classifying word problems

Expert problem solvers build up banks of images of 'archetypal' problems that serve as templates for sets of linked problems.

Classifying addition and subtraction problems

There are three main 'root' situations for addition and subtraction: combining; change; and comparison. Although the distinctions between these three are somewhat blurred, they are useful for learning at this stage.

Combining

Situations where two sets are put together to create a new set that did not previously exist are addition problems as the result of combining.

Gran gave me 10p and Granddad gave me 5p. How much do I have altogether?
(Combine 10 and 5)

I have 6 books in a pile and 10 on the shelf. I put all the books in a box.
How many books in the box?
(Combine 6 and 10 or 10 and 6)

Change (increase/decrease)

Situations where there is an initial quantity and this is increased or decreased in some way are called 'change' problems, leading either to addition or subtraction.

I have 10p in my purse and put in another 5p. How much is in my purse now?
(Change 10 by adding on 5)

I have 10 jelly beans and eat 6. How many jelly beans do I have left?
(Change 10 by taking away 6)

Although to adults it appears obvious in the first example in each case (combine and change) that the mathematical calculation is 10 + 5, to the novice learner this is not immediately obvious. As the second combine situation shows, the answer can be obtained either by adding 6 + 10 or 10 + 6. Given a similar change problem (there are 6 books in a box and I put in another 10) children are likely to want to do the calculation implied by the order of the numbers in the 'action' of the story: 6 + 10. For this reason, children are introduced to combine problems first to help them understand that addition can be done in either order.

Comparison

Situations where nothing actually changes or is combined but where two sets are compared are called 'compare' problems.

I have 10p and Penny has 5p. How much more do I have?
(What is the difference between 10 and 5?)

I have 5p and Mark has 10p. How much more do I need to have the same as Mark?
(What is the difference between 10 and 5?)

Classifying multiplication and division problems

Children are introduced to two 'root' situations for multiplication: multiplication as repeated addition and multiplication as arrays. Linked to this are two models of division: division as grouping (repeated subtraction) and division as sharing. Like addition and subtraction, the distinction between these is not firm, but the categorisation does provide a helpful model for teaching. At this stage, the children are likely to use addition and subtraction strategies for finding answers – that's fine.

Multiplication as repeated addition

Situations where several groups all the same size need to be added together are called 'multiplication as repeated addition'.

Every day for a week I put 10p into my money box. How much did I save that week?
(Add 10 to itself 7 times or multiply 10 by 7)

A packet of biscuits contains 5 biscuits. I buy 4 packets.
(Repeatedly add 5 or multiply 5 by 4)

Multiplication as arrays

'Multiplication as arrays' situations are ones where objects are set out in a rectangular pattern (cakes in tins, blocks of stamps) and the total number has to be found.

I put 10 stickers in each row and I make five rows.
How many stickers did I put on my page?
(Add 10 to itself five times, or multiply 10 by 5. Or add 5 to itself 10 times or multiply 5 by 10)

A tray of cakes has 4 rows and 5 columns. How many cakes is that altogether?
(Add 4 to itself 5 times or multiply 4 by 5. Or add 5 to itself 4 times or multiply 5 by 4)

Grouping (repeated subtraction)

Situations where an amount has to be put into equal-sized groups or portions and the size of the group or portion is known in advance are known as 'division as grouping' or 'division as repeated subtraction'.

I have picked 25 apples. I put them into bags of 5. How many bags can I fill?
(Repeatedly subtract 5 from 25 or divide 25 by 5)

I have 21 m of rope and I want to make skipping ropes that are each 3 m long. How many can I make?
(Repeatedly subtract 3 from 21 or divide 21 by 3)

Division as sharing

Situations where an amount has to be put into equal sized groups and the number of group or portion is known in advance are known as 'division as sharing'.

I have picked 15 apples. I have 5 bags to put them into.
How many apples can I put into each bag?
(Share 15 amongst 5 or divide 15 by 5)

I have 12 litres of juice and I want to put equal amounts into 6 jugs.
How much juice do I pour into each jug?
(Share 12 amongst 6 or divide 12 by 6)

Using the CD-ROM

The CD-ROM contains all the content in the Big Book. You can either project individual pages onto a whiteboard from your computer or print them out onto acetate sheets and use them on an overhead projector. The CD-ROM also contains all the problem sheets in the Teachers' Notes; this gives you the option of printing the sheets out, rather than making photocopies.

In conclusion

Throughout your work on Word Problems, it is important to be explicit with children about the different kinds of calculation involved. Children can cope with these distinctions, once you have explained the features of a calculation, and compared one problem type with another. Sharing with children what in the past has effectively been 'secret knowledge' will help them understand the mathematics and develop appropriate problem-solving skills.

Unit	Content objective	Problem-solving objective
Year 1		
1. Cats and Dogs	Understand addition problems involving combining two sets	Model addition using objects or pictures
2. Big Blue Riding Hood	Understand addition problems involving combining two sets	Model addition using objects or pictures
3. Rastpunzel	Understand addition problems involving combining two sets	Model addition using objects or pictures
4. Mermaid and merman	Understand subtraction problems involving finding the difference between two sets	Model subtraction using objects or pictures
5. Cinderfella	Understand subtraction problems involving finding the difference between two sets	Model subtraction using objects or pictures
6. Trainer life	Understand addition problems involving changing a set	Use a number track to model counting on
7. Munch time	Understand addition problems involving changing a set	Use a number track to model counting on
8. Flatz	Understand addition problems involving changing a set	Use a number track to model counting on
9. Hide and Seek	Understand subtraction problems involving taking away	Model subtraction on a number track
10. Monsters Sink	Understand subtraction problems involving taking away	Model subtraction on a number track
11. Baldilocks	Understand repeated addition problems	Model repeated addition with objects or pictures
12. Jill and Jack	Understand repeated subtraction problems	Model subtraction with objects or pictures
Year 2		
13. Circus Nights	Understand addition problems involving combining two sets	Model addition using a number line
14. On the Buses	Understand addition problems involving combining two sets	Model addition using a number line
15. The Sprats	Understand subtraction problems involving finding the difference between two sets	Model subtraction using a number line
16. Invincibles	Understand subtraction problems involving finding the difference between two sets	Model subtraction using a number line
17. Leap frogs	Understand addition problems involving increasing a set	Model addition using a number line
18. Knock, knock	Understand addition problems involving increasing a set	Model addition using a number line
19. Sleeping Ugly	Understand subtraction problems involving taking away	Model subtraction on a number line
20. Sam White	Understand subtraction problems involving taking away	Model subtraction on a number line
21. Rowdies	Understand repeated addition problems	Model repeated addition on a number line
22. Naughty Max	Understand multiplication problems	Model repeated addition as an array
23. Mama and Papa Goose	Understand division as sharing problems	Model repeated subtraction with objects or pictures
24. Mary, Mary	Understand division as repeated subtraction problems	Model division with objects or pictures

Year 1

Unit 1	**Cats and Dogs**	*14*
Unit 2	**Big Blue Riding Hood**	*16*
Unit 3	**Rastpunzel**	*18*
Unit 4	**Mermaid and merman**	*20*
Unit 5	**Cinderfella**	*22*
Unit 6	**Trainer life**	*24*
Unit 7	**Munch time**	*26*
Unit 8	**Flatz**	*28*
Unit 9	**Hide and Seek**	*30*
Unit 10	**Monsters Sink**	*32*
Unit 11	**Baldilocks**	*34*
Unit 12	**Jill and Jack**	*36*

Year 2

Unit 13	**Circus Nights**	*38*
Unit 14	**On the Buses**	*40*
Unit 15	**The Sprats**	*42*
Unit 16	**Invincibles**	*44*
Unit 17	**Leap frogs**	*46*
Unit 18	**Knock, knock**	*48*
Unit 19	**Sleeping Ugly**	*50*
Unit 20	**Sam White**	*52*
Unit 21	**Rowdies**	*54*
Unit 22	**Naughty Max**	*56*
Unit 23	**Mama and Papa Goose**	*58*
Unit 24	**Mary, Mary**	*60*

Objectives
- Understand addition problems involving combining two sets
- Model addition using objects or pictures

Big Book problems

These two problems are both addition problems. The additions are the result of 'combine' situations: two groups of objects are put together to make a third total amount. One of the advantages of starting with combine problems (as opposed to 'change' problems, where an initial amount is increased or decreased) is that children can explore whether or not it makes a difference which amount you start with. The aim of the lesson is to help children to recognise addition problems and to begin to talk about them as 'combine' situations.

Whole class

Problem 1

Talk about cats and dogs and establish the context for the problem. Do they really play well together? What do the children think the animals are going to play?

Ask the children to look at the picture. Discuss the picture and draw their attention to the line of dogs. Ask how many dogs there are. Take suggestions for how many, and talk to the children about how they counted. Did anybody see there were five and one? Encourage the children to share strategies to find out how many there are without counting in ones.

Read through the problem with the children. Encourage them to work in pairs and to use whatever means they like to find an answer. Some may choose to use objects or fingers, some may quickly draw the cats. Some may even just 'know' that $6 + 3 = 9$. In this latter case, ask the children to record something that would help a friend to understand why the answer is nine.

As the children are working on the problem, select two or three who are using different solution methods and invite them to come and share their methods with the class.

Ask if anyone can come and write a mathematical sentence for this problem and help the children record:

$6 + 3 = \square$ cats and dogs

If no one has done so, model how the answer to the question can be found by putting up six fingers and then counting on three more.

Unit 1

Problem 2

Work through the problem in the same way as the first one. In particular, look out for children who appear to be using a count-on method: starting with four and counting on two (rather than using a count-all method: putting out four fingers or objects, putting out another two and then counting from one to find that there are six).

See if anyone can record the mathematical sentence and help them set up on the board:

> 4 + 2 = ☐ cats and dogs

Linking up the problems

Ask the children to look at both problems and discuss with a partner what they have in common.

Apart from being about cats and dogs, the children should be able to notice that they are both 'add' situations. Talk about how both situations involved two amounts that needed to be put together or combined to give the final amount. Explain to the children that they are going to be making up some more problems like this.

Follow up

Pairs

Give out problem sheet A. Have sheet B in a prominent place for the children to collect later on.

As the children are working, encourage them to write down appropriate mathematical sentences.

As they finish, ask them to go and collect a copy of sheet B. Explain that they need to work with a friend to complete this sheet.

Wrap up

Whole class

Invite one or two children to come and show the others the problems that they made up and to talk about how they found the answer.

Objectives
- Understand addition problems involving combining two sets
- Model addition using objects or pictures

Big Book problems

Like the 'Cats and Dogs' problems, these two problems are both addition problems. Once again the additions are the result of 'combining' situations: two groups of objects are put together to make a third total amount. As before, one aim of the lesson is to help children to recognise addition problems and to begin to talk about them as 'combine' problems.

Whole class

Problem 1

Talk about Big Blue Riding Hood and establish the context for the problem. How does this compare with Little Red Riding Hood?

Ask the children to look at the picture. Discuss the picture and draw their attention to the apples in the basket that contains five. Ask how many apples there are. Take suggestions for how many, and talk to the children about how they counted. Did anybody notice the pattern of five.

Read through the problem with the children. Encourage them to work in pairs and to use whatever means they like to find an answer. Some may choose to use objects or fingers, some may quickly draw the apples. Some may even just 'know' that $5 + 1 = 6$. In this latter case, ask the children to record something that would help a friend to understand why the answer is six.

As the children are working on the problem, select two or three who are using different solution methods and invite them to come and share their methods with the class.

Ask if anyone can come and write a mathematical sentence for this problem and help the children record:

$5 + 1 = \square$ apples

If no one has done so, model how the answer to the question can be found by putting up five fingers on one hand and one on the other and seeing that there are six altogether.

Unit 2

Problem 2

Work through the problem in the same way as the first one. In particular, look out for children who appear to choose to start with four and to add on two (rather than two add on four as suggested by the order of the numbers in the question).

See if anyone can record the mathematical sentence and help them set up on the board:

$2 + 4 = \square$ pies

Under this, record:

$4 + 2 = \square$ pies

Who thinks the answer to this will be the same? Who thinks it will be different?
Invite two children to the front. Ask one to hold up two fingers (or two objects) and the other to hold up four. Establish that there are six fingers altogether. Swap the position of the two children but each still holds up the same number of fingers. Has the total number of fingers changed?

Linking up the problems

Ask the children to look at both problems and discuss with a partner what they have in common.

Apart from being about the objects in the baskets, the children should be able to notice that they are both 'add' situations. Talk about how both situations involved two amounts that needed to be put together or combined to give the final amount. Explain to the children that they are going to be making up some more problems like this.

Follow up

Pairs

Give out problem sheet A. Have sheet B in a prominent place for the children to collect later on. While the children are working, encourage them to write down appropriate mathematical sentences. As they finish, ask them to go and collect a copy of sheet B.

Wrap up

Whole class

Whose friend made up a hard problem? Were they able to solve it?

Objectives
- Understand addition problems involving combining two sets
- Model addition using objects or pictures

Big Book problems

Here again, the two problems are both addition problems. The additions are the result of 'combine' situations: two groups of objects are put together to make a third total amount. Building on the first two units, the aim of the lesson is to further develop children's ability to recognise addition problems and to talk about them as 'combine' problems.

Whole class

Problem 1

Talk about Rastpunzel and establish the context for the problem. Has anyone heard the story of Rapunzel? Why is her hair important in the story? Check that everyone knows what a comb is.

Ask the children to look at the picture. Discuss the picture and draw their attention to the combs in the drawer. Ask how many red combs there are. Take suggestions for how many, and talk to the children about how they counted. Did anybody see there were five and two? Encourage the children to share strategies to find out how many there are withou counting in ones.

Read through the problem with the children. Encourage them to work in pairs and to use whatever means they like to find an answer. Some may choose to use objects or fingers, some may quickly draw the combs. Some may even just 'know' that 7 + 3 = 10. In this latter case, ask the children to record something that would help a friend to understand why the answer is ten.

As the children are working on the problem, select two or three who are using different solution methods and invite them to come and share their methods with the class.

Ask if anyone can come and write a mathematical sentence for this problem and help the children record:

7 + 3 = ☐ combs

If no one has do so, model how the answer to the question can be found by putting up seven fingers on one hand and three on the other and seeing that there are ten altogether.

Problem 2

Work through the problem in the same way as the first one. In particular look out for children who appear to choose to start with eight and to add on two (rather than two add on eight as suggested by the order of the numbers in the question).

See if anyone can record the mathematical sentence and help them set up on the board:

$2 + 8 = \square$ hats

Under this, record:

$8 + 2 = \square$ hats

Who thinks the answer to this will be the same? Who thinks it will be different? Invite two children to the front. Ask one to hold up two fingers (or two objects) and the other to hold up eight. Establish that there are ten fingers altogether. Swap the position of the two children but each child still holds up the same number of fingers. Has the total number of fingers changed?

Linking up the problems

Ask the children to look at both problems and discuss with a partner what they have in common.

Apart from being about combs and hats, the children should be able to notice that they are both 'add' situations. Talk about how both situations involved two amounts that needed to be put together or combined to give the final amount. Explain to the children that they are going to be making up some more problems like this.

Follow up

Pairs

Give out problem sheet A. Have sheet B in a prominent place for the children to collect later on. As the children are working, encourage them to write down appropriate mathematical sentences. As they finish, ask them to go and collect a copy of sheet B. Explain that they need to work with a friend to complete this sheet.

Wrap up

Whole class

Invite one or two children to come and show the others the problems that they made up and to talk about how they found the answer.

Objectives
- Understand subtraction problems involving finding the difference between two sets
- Model subtraction using objects or pictures

Big Book problems

The two problems here are both subtraction problems. The subtractions are the result of 'compare' situations: two groups of objects are compared to find the difference. Usually children's first experience of subtraction is 'take away'. But comparing is easier as it follows on from looking at 'combine' problems in that there are two quantities initially. In finding the difference problems, both quantities remain visible, so children can find the answer by matching up sets of objects and 'seeing' or counting by how many more one set is larger than the other. The aim of the lesson is to begin to develop children's ability to recognise subtraction problems and to talk about them as 'compare' or 'difference' problems.

Whole class

Problem 1

Talk about merpeople and establish the context for the problem. Explain that Ethel and Eddie are playing a game with shells and they have to decide who has the most shells or stars.

Ask the children to look at the picture. Discuss the picture and draw their attention to the shells in front of Ethel and Eddie Ask how many shells Ethel has. Take suggestions for how many, and talk to the children about how they counted. Did anybody 'see' that there were five and one and put these together to get six? Encourage the children to share strategies to find out how many there are without counting in ones.

Repeat the procedure with Eddie's shells. Recap how many shells each merperson has. Ask the children to turn to a partner and to see if they can decide who has the most shells. Bring the class together and check that they know that Ethel has more shells.

Ask them to turn to their partner again and to see if they can figure out how many more shells Ethel has. Encourage them to use whatever means they like to find an answer. Some may choose to use objects or fingers, some may quickly draw the shells. Some may even just 'know' that the difference is one. In this latter case, ask the children to record something that would help a friend to understand why the answer is ten.

As the children are working on the problem, select two or three who are using different solution methods and invite them to come and share their methods with the class.

Draw the children's attention to the way the shells are arranged: Ethel has a row of five and one over, Eddie simply has a row of five. So we can see that Ethel has one more.

Unit 4

It is unlikely that the children will know how to record this in a mathematical sentence, so put up two ways of recording it and talk through each one:

$$5 + 1 = 6$$

$$6 - 1 = 5$$

The intention here is not that children should begin to use subtraction notation independently – it is simply to expose them to the notation.

Problem 2

Work through the problem in the same way as the first one. It is not quite so easy to 'see' the difference between four and seven. Work on how the children could think about adding one more to four to make five, then two more to make seven. Having two sticks of interlocking cubes, one four long and one seven long (made of five in one colour and two in a second) and 'building up' the four in these two stages to seven will help the children see the difference and how to think about it.

Again, don't expect the children to be able to record this in a mathematical sentence, so put up two ways of recording it and talk through each one:

$$4 + 3 = 7$$

$$7 - 3 = 4$$

Linking up the problems

Ask the children to look at both problems and discuss with a partner what they have in common. Apart from being about shells and stars, the children should be able to notice that they are both 'compare' situations. Talk about how both situations involved two amounts that needed to be compared to see which was bigger and by how much. Explain to the children that they are going to be making up some more problems like this.

Follow up

Pairs

Give out problem sheet A. Have sheet B in a prominent place for the children to collect later on. As the children are working, encourage them to write down whatever mathematical sentences they think are appropriate. As they finish, ask them to go and collect a copy of sheet B.

Wrap up

Whole class

Make up one or two similar problems to pose orally to the class. Who can explain how they figured out the answer?

Objectives
- Understand subtraction problems involving finding the difference between two sets
- Model subtraction using objects or pictures

Big Book problems

As in the previous unit, the two problems here are both subtraction problems. Once again the subtractions are the result of 'compare' situations: two groups of objects are compared to find the difference. The aim of the lesson is to further develop children's ability to recognise subtraction problems and to talk about them as 'compare' or 'difference' problems.

Whole class

Problem 1

Talk about Cinderfella and establish the context for the problem. How does this story compare with the story of Cinderella?

Ask the children to look at the picture. Discuss the picture and draw their attention to the fact that Harry has some boots and Cinderfella has some boots, too. Explain that you want them to look at the picture and decide how many boots Cinderfella has. Take suggestions for how many, and talk to the children about how they counted. Did anybody see there were five and four?

Repeat this with procedure with Harry's boots. Again, draw their attention to the structure of five and one to help them know quickly that there are six altogether. Recap how many boots each brother has. Ask the children to turn to a partner and to see if they can decide who has the most boots. Bring the class together and check that they know that Cinderfella has more boots. Record 9 and 6 to remind the children of how many boots there are.

Ask them to turn to their partner again and to see if they can figure out how many more boots Cinderfella has. Encourage them to use whatever means they like to find an answer. Some may choose to use objects or fingers, some may quickly draw the boots. Some may even just 'know' that the difference is three. In this latter case, ask the children to record something that would help a friend understand why the answer is three.

As the children are working on the problem, select two or three who are using different solution methods and invite them to come and share their methods with the class.

Draw the children's attention to the way the boots are arranged: Cinderfella has a row of five and four over, Harry has a row of five and one over. So we only need to look at the boots in the second row in each case. Then we can see that Cinderfella has three more.

Put up two ways of recording it and talk through each one:

22

Unit 5

$$6 + 3 = 9$$

$$9 - 3 = 6$$

Leave both of these number sentences up on the board to refer to later.

Problem 2

Work through the problem in the same way as the first one. It is not quite so easy to 'see' the difference between nine and three. Work on how the children could think about adding two more to three to make five, then four more to make nine. Having two sticks of interlocking cubes, one three long and one nine long (made of five in one colour and four in a second) and 'building up' the three in these two stages to nine will help the children see the difference and how to think about it.

Again, don't expect the children to be able to record this in a mathematical sentence. Put up two ways of recording it and talk through each one:

$$3 + 6 = 9$$

$$9 - 3 = 6$$

Draw the children's attention to the sentences on the board from the first problem. Can they see any connection or pattern?

Linking up the problems

Ask the children to look at both problems and discuss with a partner what they have in common.

Apart from being about brothers, the children should be able to notice that they are both 'compare' situations. Talk about how both situations involved two amounts that needed to be compared to see which was bigger and by how much. Explain to the children that they are going to be making up some more problems like this.

Follow up

Pairs

Give out problem sheet A. Have sheet B in a prominent place for the children to collect later on. As the children are working, encourage them to write down whatever mathematical sentences they think are appropriate. As they finish, ask them to go and collect a copy of sheet B.

Wrap up

Whole class

Invite one or two children to come and show the others the problems that they made up and to talk about how they found the answer.

Objectives
- Understand addition problems involving changing a set
- Use a number track to model counting on

Big Book problems

This unit returns to addition situations. Previously the children have worked on situations that result in addition from combining two separate sets. Here the additions are the result of slightly different types of contexts: a single set is changed and made larger. So we are given the initial quantity, the size of the change and the final resultant size set has to be found. These types of contexts encourage children to use counting on strategies to find a solution (as opposed to counting all strategies), so they are introduced to the use of a number track to help them find the answers.

Whole class

Problem 1

Talk about the old woman who lived in the shoe and establish the context for the problem. What is different about this version? What is the same?

Ask the children to look at the picture. Discuss the picture and draw their attention to mother mouse dishing supper up for the young mice. Ask the children how many mice are sitting at the table. Take suggestions for how many, and talk to the children about how they counted. Did anybody see there were five and one?

Read through the problem with the children. Encourage them to work in pairs and to use whatever means they like to find an answer. Some may choose to use objects or fingers, some may quickly draw the mice. Some may even just 'know' that 6 + 4 = 10. In this latter case, ask the children to record something that would help a friend to understand why the answer is ten.

As the children are working on the problem, select two or three who are using different solution methods and invite them to come and share their methods with the class.

Ask if anyone can come and write a mathematical sentence for this problem and help the children record:

    6 + 4 = ☐ mice

Leave this on the board to refer to later.

Model how to find the answer to the question by starting on 6 on a number track and counting on 4 to 10.

Unit 6

Problem 2

Work through the problem in a similar way as the first one. Start by establishing that four mice have gone to bed. Establish that six more are lined up in the picture and record that there are six.

As they work on finding an answer, look out for children who appear to realise that they can use the answer to the first problem to find the answer to this one.

See if anyone can record the mathematical sentence and help them set up on the board:

$4 + 6 = \square$ mice

Direct the children back to $6 + 4$. Can anyone explain why the answer to the two problems is the same?

Model how to find the answer to the question by starting on 6 on the number track and counting on 4 to 10.

Linking up the problems

Ask the children to look at both problems and discuss with a partner what they have in common.

Apart from being about mice, the children should be able to notice that they are both 'add' situations. Talk about how both situations involved an initial number of mice – six at the table, four gone to bed – and that this amounts was changed or increased in some way – more mice arriving, more mice going to bed. Explain to the children that they are going to be making up some more problems like this.

Follow up

Pairs

Give out problem sheet A. Have sheet B in a prominent place for the children to collect later on. As the children are working, encourage them to write down appropriate mathematical sentences. As they finish, ask them to go and collect a copy of sheet B. Explain that they need to work with a friend to complete this sheet.

Wrap up

Whole class

Invite one or two children to come and show the others the answer to one of the problems from sheet B. Can the class suggest what the problem might have been?

25

Objectives
- Understand addition problems involving changing a set
- Use a number track to model counting on

Big Book problems

This unit builds on the previous one and provides further addition as change situations. Such situations are helpful in encouraging children to use counting on strategies (instead of counting all strategies), and larger numbers are used here to further encourage this. The use of a number track is also used to model counting on strategies.

Whole class

Problem 1

Read through the first verse of the rhyme with the children – repeat it and encourage them to join in.

Ask the children to look at the picture. Discuss the picture and draw their attention to the array of apples. Ask how many apples there are. Take suggestions for how many, and talk to the children about how they counted. Did anybody 'see' the five in each row, and that there were three rows? As a reminder, record that there are 15 apples.

Read through the second verse with the children. Check that everyone knows that Maisie eats some more apples – 3 more than the 15 she has already eaten. Encourage them to work in pairs and to use whatever means they like to find an answer.

As the children are working on the problem, select two or three who are using different solution methods and invite them to come and share their methods with the class.

Ask if anyone can come and write a mathematical sentence for this problem and help the children record:

15 + 3 = ☐ apples

Leave this on the board to refer to later.

Model how the answer to the question by starting on 15 on a number track and counting on 3 to 18.

Problem 2

Work through the problem in a similar way as the first one. Start by establishing that there are 14 carrots. Did anyone spot that this had to be one fewer than the 15 because there was one fewer carrot in the last row? Get someone to record 14 on the cover as a reminder.

Unit 7

As they work on finding an answer, look out for children who appear to realise that they can use the answer to the first problem to find the answer to this one.

See if anyone can record the mathematical sentence and help them set up on the board:

14 + 4 = ☐ carrots

Direct the children back to 15 + 3. Can anyone explain why the answer to the two problems is the same? Discuss with them that since the 14 is one fewer than 15 but 4 is one more than 3 then the answer must be the same. Model this with counters or cubes.

Model how the answer to the question by starting on 14 on the number track and counting on 4 to 18.

Linking up the problems

Ask the children to look at both problems and discuss with a partner what they have in common.

Apart from being about a donkey eating food, the children should be able to notice that they are both 'add' situations. Talk about how both situations involved an initial number of apples or carrots and that this amount was changed or increased in some way. Explain to the children that they are going to be making up some more problems like this.

Follow up

Pairs

Give out problem sheet A. Have sheet B in a prominent place for the children to collect later on. As the children are working, encourage them to write down appropriate mathematical sentences. As they finish, ask them to go and collect a copy of sheet B. Explain that they need to work with a friend to complete this sheet.

Wrap up

Whole class

Make up one or two similar problems to pose orally to the class. Who can explain how they figured out the answer?

Objectives
- Understand addition problems involving changing a set
- Use a number track to model counting on

Big Book problems

This unit builds on the previous one and provides further addition as change situations. However, the structure of the problems in this unit makes them considerably harder for children to make sense of. In the previous two units an initial amount was given and the size of the change provided. The children then had to work out the final total. In this unit the initial and final quantities are given and the children have to find the size of the change. The intention here is merely to expose the children to this structure. Do not expect them to fully understand it at this stage.

Whole class

Problem 1

Talk about the context with the children. Do the Flatz dolls remind them of anything?

Ask the children to look at the picture. Discuss the picture and draw their attention to the lines of Flatz dancing. Ask how many Flatz there are. Explain that there won't be enough time to count them, so the children are going to have to look carefully and see if they can tell how many Flatz there are without counting in ones. Take suggestions for how many, and talk to the children about how they counted. By now, children should be able to 'see' the five in each row and that there were two rows.

Read through the problem with the children. It may take some discussion for the children to be clear that the situation is that 15 Flatz have ended up on the dance floor and not that 15 more got up to dance. One way to help the children appreciate the situation is to get them to retell the problem in their own words. Set the children off to figure out how many Flatz got up to dance.

As the children are working on the problem, select two or three who are using different solution methods and invite them to come and share their methods with the class.

Model how the answer to the question can be found by locating 10 on a number track and counting on until you get to 15.

Write up the following mathematical sentence for this problem:

$10 + \square = 15$

Leave this on the board to refer to later.

Unit 8

Problem 2

Work through the problem in a similar way as the first one. Start by establishing that there are 4 Flatz having a drink. Once again, make sure that the children are clear that after some time there are 14 Flatz having a drink and that the children have to figure out how many joined the 4.

Model how the answer to the question by starting on 4 on the number track and counting on to 14 and counting the number of jumps.

Direct the children back to the mathematical sentence for the first problem. Can anyone can record a similar mathematical sentence for this problem? Help them set up on the board:

$$4 + \square = 14$$

Linking up the problems

Discuss with the children that these are change problems like the ones that they have been working on, Refer back to the problems in the previous two units and recap that the problems there involved a quantity – mice or apples and carrots – that was changed in some way – made bigger. Talk about how these problems were similar but that here they had to work out what the change was. Explain to the children that they are going to be making up some more problems like this.

Follow up

Pairs

Give out problem sheet A. Have sheet B in a prominent place for the children to collect later on. As the children are working, encourage them to write down appropriate mathematical sentences. As they finish, ask them to go and collect a copy of sheet B. Explain that they need to work with a friend to complete this sheet.

Wrap up

Whole class

Invite one or two children to come and tell the others the answer to one of the problems that they made up. Can the class come up with suggestions for what the problem might have been?

Objectives
- Understand subtraction problems involving taking away
- Model subtraction on a number track

Big Book problems

The two problems here are both subtraction problems. The subtractions are the result of 'change' situations: an initial quantity is changed by something being removed. This is the popular interpretation of subtraction as taking away. These problems link to addition as change problems, but here the change is a decrease rather than an increase. The aim of the lesson is to begin to develop children's ability to recognise subtraction problems and to talk about them as 'change' or 'take away' problems.

Whole class

Problem 1

Talk about the context for the problem. Does anyone know the rhyme about elephants on a spider's web?

Ask the children to look at the picture. Discuss the picture and draw their attention to the elephants on the spider's web. By now, the children should be familiar with the routine of how they need to decide how many things are in the picture, but without counting them all. Ask how many elephants there are. Take suggestions for how many, and talk to the children about how they counted. Did anybody see there were five in each row, with three rows, and one over? Record 16 as a reminder of how many elephants there are.

Go over the problem with the children. Make sure that everyone is clear that two elephants from the 16 went off to hide and that the children have to figure out how many were left playing on the spider's web. You might want to model this using counters or cubes; get a child to count 16 cubes into an opaque container and then get another child to take two cubes out. The children have to figure out how many cubes are left in the container.

As the children are working on the problem, select two or three who are using different solution methods and invite them to come and share their methods with the class.

Some children may know how to record this in a mathematical sentence. Help them record it using the subtraction symbol:

$$16 - 2 = 14$$

Leave this on the board to refer to later.

Model how to solve this using a number track by locating 16 and counting back 2 to 14.

Problem 2

Work through the problem in the same way as the first one. As with the first problem, use a 'brief look' to establish that there are 17 spiders. Again, it might help to model the problem using counters or cubes and a container.

Once one or two children have shared their methods and answers, work with them on recording the appropriate subtraction sentence:

$$17 - 2 = 15$$

Draw the children's attention back to the sentence 16 – 2. Can anyone see a connection or pattern between the two sentences.

Again, model solving the second problem using the number track.

Linking up the problems

Ask the children to look at both problems and discuss with a partner what they have in common.

Apart from being about spiders and elephants, the children should be able to notice that they are both 'take away' situations. Talk about how both situations involved a starting amount that was changed by something being removed or taken away. Explain to the children that they are going to be solving some more problems like this.

Follow up

Pairs

Give out problem sheet A. Have sheet B in a prominent place for the children to collect later on. As the children are working, encourage them to write down whatever mathematical sentences they think are appropriate. As they finish, ask them to go and collect a copy of sheet B.

Wrap up

Whole class

Make up one or two similar problems to pose orally to the class. Who can explain how they figured out the answer?

Objectives
- Understand subtraction problems involving taking away
- Model subtraction on a number track

Big Book problems

The two problems here are again both subtraction problems. The aim of the lesson is to further develop children's ability to recognise subtraction problems and to talk about them as 'change' or 'take away' problems. Although the numbers here are smaller than in the previous unit, taking a single digit away from ten is more challenging than taking a digit away from a teen number.

Whole class

Problem 1

Talk about the context for the problem. What does the title remind them of?

By now, the children should be expecting the routine of being asked to decide how many things they can see, but without counting them all. Discuss the picture and draw their attention to the 'earwigs' swimming in the bath. Ask how many earwigs there are. Take suggestions for how many, and talk to the children about how they counted. Did anybody see that there were five in each lane and that there were two lanes? Record the number 10 to act as a reminder of how many earwigs there are.

Go over the problem with the children. Make sure that everyone is clear that two earwigs from the 10 in the picture leave the bath and that the children have to figure out how many would still be swimming. You might want to model this using counters or cubes; get a child to count 10 cubes into an opaque container and then get another child to take two cubes out. The children have to figure out how many cubes are left in the container.

As the children are working on the problem, select two or three who are using different solution methods and invite them to come and share their methods with the class.

Some children may know how to record this in a mathematical sentence. Help them record it using the subtraction symbol:

$$10 - 2 = 8$$

Leave this on the board to refer to later.

Unit 10

Problem 2

Work through the problem in the same way as the first one. As in the first problem, use the 'brief look' to establish that there are 10 eyelashes. Again it might help to model the problem using counters or cubes and a container.

Once one or two children have shared their methods and answers, work with them on recording the appropriate subtraction sentence:

$$10 - 3 = 7$$

Draw the children's attention back to the sentence 10 − 2. Can anyone see a connection or pattern between the two sentences? Did anyone use the answer to the first problem to find the answer to the second one?

Linking up the problems

Ask the children to look at both problems and discuss with a partner what they have in common.

Apart from being about surreal creatures, the children should be able to notice that they are both 'take away' situations. Talk about how both situations involved a starting amount that was changed by something being removed or taken away. Explain to the children that they are going to be solving some more problems like this.

Follow up

Pairs

Give out problem sheet A. Have sheet B in a prominent place for the children to collect later on. As the children are working, encourage them to write down whatever mathematical sentences they think are appropriate. As they finish, ask them to go and collect a copy of sheet B.

Wrap up

Whole class

Invite one or two children to come and show the others the problems that they made up and to talk about how they found the answer.

Objectives
- Understand repeated addition problems
- Model repeated addition with objects or pictures

Big Book problems

This unit and the one that follows begin, in a simple way, to explore the origins of multiplication and division. Multiplication is introduced here through a context requiring repeated addition. The intention is not that children should themselves begin to use the notation of multiplication to represent repeated addition. It is simply that they are exposed to the notation.

Whole class

Problem 1

Talk about the context for the problem. Does Baldilocks remind them of anybody? Who? What is similar and what is different?

Go over the problem with the children. You might want to model the situation using counters or cubes; this has to be done in such a way as to discourage children from counting all the objects and to encourage them, if they can, to work with mental images. So you might use containers instead of chairs or put chairs with 'cushions' (counters) at a distance too far for the children to see the 'cushions' on the chair. In either case, the children should be involved in placing three 'cushions' on each chair, and checking that each holds the same. The children have to figure out how many 'cushions' that there are altogether.

Although the model of the problem needs to be set up in such a way that the children cannot easily see all the 'cushions' when they come to work it out for themselves, do allow those children who need to represent all three sets to do so, by using objects, or making sketches. As usual, select two or three who are using different solution methods and invite them to come and share their methods with the class.

Some children may be unsure over whether this can be recorded using the addition symbol. If they have only previously experienced adding two objects together, then they may think that using two addition symbols in a number sentence is 'against the rules'. Work on setting up the sentence:

$$3 + 3 + 3 = 9$$

Explain to the children that there is another way of recording this situation:

$$3 \times 3 = 9 \text{ (read as 'three multiplied by three equals nine')}$$

Leave this on the board to refer to later.

Problem 2

Work through the problem in the same way as the first one. Again, set up the situation with physical objects that are hidden from view once set out.

Once one or two children have shared their methods and answers, work with them on recording the appropriate addition sentence:

$5 + 5 + 5 = 15$

Set up the multiplicative way of recording this:

$5 \times 3 = 15$ (read as 'five multiplied by three equals fifteen')

Draw the children's attention back to the sentence $3 \times 3 = 9$. Point out the similarities in the way the two sentences are constructed and read.

Linking up the problems

Ask the children to look at both problems and discuss with a partner what they have in common.

Apart from being about food for the bears, the children should be able to notice that they are both 'add' situations where three things are added. Explain to the children that they are going to be solving some more problems like this.

Follow up

Pairs

Give out problem sheet A. Have sheet B in a prominent place for the children to collect later on. As the children are working, encourage them to write down whatever mathematical sentences they think are appropriate. As they finish, ask them to go and collect a copy of sheet B. Tell them they need a friend to help.

Wrap up

Whole class

Make up one or two similar problems to pose orally to the class. Who can explain how they figured out the answer?

Objectives
- Understand repeated subtraction problems
- Model subtraction with objects or pictures

Big Book problems

This unit introduces, in a very simple way, the origin of division as repeated subtraction. The intention is not that children should themselves begin to use the notation of division to represent repeated subtraction. It is simply that they are exposed to the notation.

Whole class

Problem 1

Talk about the context for the problem. Does anyone know the the nursery rhyme 'Jack and Jill'. Explain that Jill is taking water from the well and putting it into buckets and that she is putting the same number of buckets into each box.

By now, the children should be expecting the routine of how they need to decide how many things there are, but without counting them all. Ask the children to look at the picture. Discuss the picture and draw their attention to the buckets of water at the top of the picture. By now the children should be familiar with the routine of needing to decide how many things are under the covers, but without counting them all. Ask how many buckets they think there are. Point to the top row of buckets and make sure everyone is clear that there are four buckets in the row. Explain to the children that each row originally had the same number of buckets, but that Jill has put some in a box.

Check that everyone is clear that Jill filled twelve buckets with water and she is putting four into each box. The children have to figure out how many boxes, each containing four buckets, Jill can fill.

Children may need to model this with counters or cubes.

Go over the problem solution with the children. You might want to model the situation using counters or cubes; counting out 12 and taking away groups of 4 to put into bags. Once everyone is clear that 3 bags are filled, refer their attention back to the picture. Did the way the buckets are laid out on the ground help anyone find the answer? Draw the children's attention to the fact that there are four buckets in each row, so each row can be used to fill a box. There are three rows, so three boxes are needed.

Unit 12

Problem 2

Work through the problem in the same way as the first one.

Once one or two children have shared their methods and answers, work with them on the fact that there were four bottles in each row, there were three rows, so three boxes are needed.

Linking up the problems

Ask the children to look at both problems and discuss with a partner what they have in common.

Apart from being about getting water from the well, the children should begin to be able to talk about them both being 'take away' situations where three things are subtracted. Explain to the children that they are going to be solving some more problems like this.

Follow up

Pairs

Give out problem sheet A. Have sheet B in a prominent place for the children to collect later on. As the children are working, encourage them to write down whatever mathematical sentences they think are appropriate. As they finish, ask them to go and collect a copy of sheet B.

Wrap up

Whole class

Invite one or two children to come and show the others the problems that they made up and to talk about how they found the answer.

Objectives
- Understand addition problems involving combining two sets
- Model addition using a number line

Big Book problems

The two problems here are both addition problems. The additions are the result of 'combine' situations: two groups of objects are put together to make a third total amount. The other situation that results in addition are 'change' problems, where an initial amount is increased or decreased. The advantage of combine problems is that children can explore whether or not it makes a difference which group you start with (the commutative law).

Whole class

Problem 1

Talk about the circus and establish the context for the problem. Has anyone ever seen somebody juggling with plates?

Read through the problem with the children. Encourage them to work in pairs and to use whatever means they like to find an answer. Some may need to count on in ones from 46, some may use the fact that they know that 6 + 3 = 9, some may even just 'know' that the answer is 49. In this latter case, ask the children to record something that would help a friend to understand why that is the answer.

As the children are working on the problem, select two or three who are using different solution methods and invite them to come and share their methods with the class.

Ask if anyone can come and write a mathematical sentence for this problem and help the children record:

$$46 + 3 = \square$$

If no one has done so, model how the answer to the question can be found by using an empty number line.

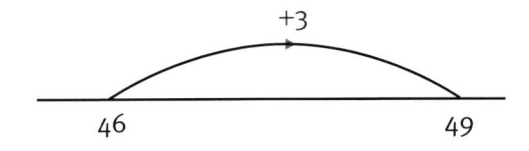

Unit 13

Problem 2

Work through the problem in the same way as the first one. In particular, look out for children who choose to start with 54 and to add on four (rather than four add on 54 as suggested by the order of the numbers in the question).

See if anyone can record the mathematical sentence and help them set up on the board:

4 + 54 = ☐

Under this, record:

54 + 4 = ☐

Who thinks the answer to this will be the same? Who thinks it will be different? Model each on the empty number line:

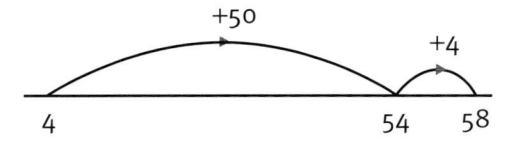

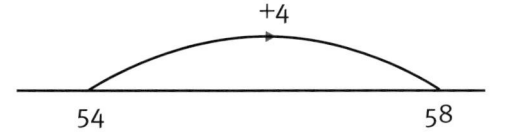

[Number line diagram: from 4, jump +50 to 54, then +4 to 58. Second number line: from 54, jump +4 to 58.]

Which method do the children think is easier?

Linking up the problems

Ask the children to look at both problems and discuss with a partner what they have in common.

Apart from being about jugglers, the children should be able to identify that they are both 'add' situations. Talk about how both situations involved two amounts that needed to be put together or combined to give the final amount. Explain to the children that they are going to be solving some more problems like this.

Follow up

Pairs

Give out problem sheet A. Have sheet B in a prominent place for the children to collect later on. As the children are working, encourage them to write down appropriate mathematical sentences. As they finish, ask them to go and collect a copy of sheet B. Explain that they need a friend to help.

Wrap up

Whole class

Invite one or two children to come and show the others the problems that they made up and to talk about how they found the answer.

Objectives
- Understand addition problems involving combining two sets
- Model addition using a number line

Big Book problems

Like the 'Circus Nights' problems, these two problems are addition problems. Once again, the additions are the result of 'combine' situations: two groups of objects are put together to make a third total amount. As before, one aim of the lesson is to help children to recognise addition problems and to begin to talk about them as 'combine' problems.

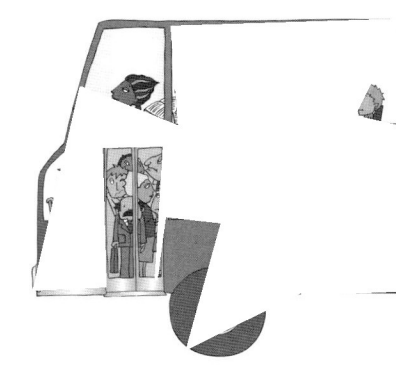

Whole class

Problem 1

Talk about traveling on buses to establish the context for the problem. Which number buses do the children go on? Where do they go to?

Read through the problem with the children. Encourage them to work in pairs and to use whatever means they like to find an answer. Some may need to count on in ones from 80, some may just 'know' that the answer is 87. In this latter case, ask the children to record something that would help a friend to understand why that is the answer.

As the children are working on the problem, watch out for any children who say they need to use the number 38 in their calculation. Talk with them about the meaning of the various numbers in the story and which ones are relevant and why.

Select two or three who are using different solution methods and invite them to come and share their methods with the class.

Ask if anyone can come and write a mathematical sentence for this problem and help the children record:

$$80 + 7 = \square$$

Discuss with the children why this is an 'easy' calculation that they should be able to answer without counting on in ones from 80.

Problem 2

Work through the problem in the same way as the first one. In particular, look out for children who choose to start with 60 and to add on five (rather than five add on 60 as suggested by the order of the numbers in the question).

See if anyone can record the mathematical sentence and help them set up on the board:

$5 + 60 = \square$

Under this, record:

$60 + 5 = \square$

Who thinks the answer to this will be the same? Who thinks it will be different? Which calculations do the children think is the easier to answer?

Linking up the problems

Ask the children to look at both problems and discuss with a partner what they have in common.

Apart from being about buses, the children should be able to notice that they are both 'add' situations. Talk about how both situations involved two amounts that needed to be put together or combined to give the final amount. Explain to the children that they are going to be solving some more problems like this.

Follow up

Pairs

Give out problem sheet A. Have sheet B in a prominent place for the children to collect later on.

As the children are working, encourage them to write down appropriate mathematical sentences.

As they finish, ask them to go and collect a copy of sheet B. Explain that they need to work with a friend to complete this sheet.

Wrap up

Whole class

Whose friend made up a hard problem? Were they able to solve it?

Objectives
- Understand subtraction problems involving finding the difference between two sets
- Model subtraction using a number line

Big Book problems

Both problems are subtraction problems. The subtractions are the result of 'compare' situations: two groups of objects are compared to find the difference. Comparing in this way follows on from looking at 'combine' problems. The aim of the lesson is to continue to develop children's ability to recognise subtraction problems and to talk about them as 'compare' or 'difference' problems and relate this to the notation for subtraction.

Whole class

Problem 1

Talk about Jack and Jill Sprat to establish the context for the problem. Who has heard the rhyme that begins 'Jack Sprat could eat no fat...'?

Ask the children to look at the picture. Discuss the picture and make clear that Jack has to eat 68 raisins and that the first picture also shows the number of raisins that Jill can eat. Ask the children to look at the picture and decide how many raisins Jill has. Take suggestions for how many, and confirm that there are five.

Ask them to turn to their partner again and to see if they can figure out how many more raisins Jack ate than Jill. The structure of the problem means that some children are likely to find the answer by counting on from 5 to 68. Encourage them to use an empty number line to keep track.

It is also likely that some children will want to add 68 and 5. You can help them appreciate the problem by setting up a physical model of the situation: put a lot of counters or cubes in one bag (there does not have to be exactly 68 – the counters are there to help the children get a sense of the situation rather than to use them to solve the problem). Put five counters in another bag. Get two children to be Jack and Jill each with a bag of 'raisins'. Go over the problem, establishing that they have to figure out how many more raisins there are in Jack's bag than in Jill's.

As the children are working on the problem, select two or three who are using different solution methods and invite them to come and share their methods with the class.

Discuss with the children that there are two ways to record this in a mathematical sentence :

$5 + \square = 68$

$68 - 5 = \square$

Unit 15

Model each of these on an empty number line and discuss which is easier to do.

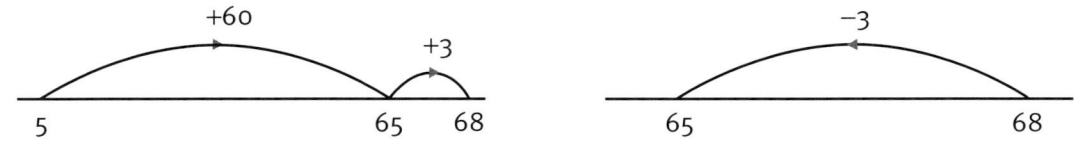

```
        +60              +3                              −3
     ⌒              ⌒                        ⌒
  5            65    68                  65              68
```

Also model on the number line how the five could be split to make the jump back from 68 in two steps.

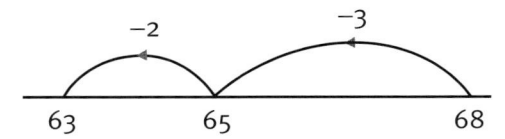

```
        −2        −3
     ⌒       ⌒
  63      65       68
```

Problem 2

Work through the problem in the same way as the first one..

Again, put up two ways of recording it and talk through each one using the empty number line to model solution strategies:

$4 + \square = 86$

$86 - 4 = \square$

Linking up the problems

Ask the children to look at both problems and discuss with a partner what they have in common.

Apart from being about peanuts and raisins, the children should be able to notice that they are both 'compare' situations. Talk about how both situations involved two amounts that needed to be compared to see which was bigger and by how much. Explain to the children that they are going to be solving some more problems like this.

Follow up

Pairs

Give out problem sheet A. Have sheet B in a prominent place for the children to collect later on. As the children are working, encourage them to write down whatever mathematical sentences they think are appropriate. As they finish, ask them to go and collect a copy of sheet B. They need a friend to help.

Wrap up

Whole class

Invite one or two children to come and show the others the problems that they made up and to talk about how they found the answer.

43

Objectives

- Understand subtraction problems involving finding the difference between two sets
- Model subtraction using a number line

Big Book problems

As in the previous unit, the two problems here are both subtraction problems. Once again, the subtractions are the result of 'compare' situations: two groups of objects are compared to find the difference. The aim of the lesson is to further develop children's ability to recognise subtraction problems and to talk about them as 'compare' or 'difference' problems.

Whole class

Problem 1

Talk about Max Maxi and Steph Stretch to establish the context for the problem. Do these superheroes remind the children of any cartoon characters?

Ask the children to look at the picture. How many dogs can Norm carry? Ask them to turn to their partner and see if they can figure out how many more dogs Max can carry than Norm. It is likely that some children will want to add 100 and 5. You can help them appreciate the problem by setting up a physical model of the situation: put a lot of counters or cubes in one bag (there does not have to be exactly 100. Put five counters in another bag. Get two children to be Max and Norm each carrying their 'dogs'. Go over the problem, establishing that they have to figure out how many more dogs there are in Max's bag than in Norm's.

As the children are working on the problem, select two or three who are using different solution methods and invite them to come and share their methods with the class.

Discuss with the children that there are two ways to record this in a mathematical sentence :

$5 + \square = 100$

$100 - 5 = \square$

Model each of these on an empty number line and discuss which is easier to do.

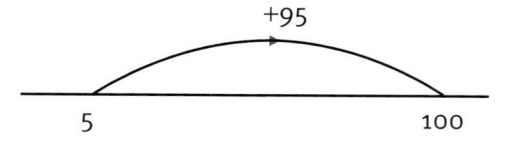

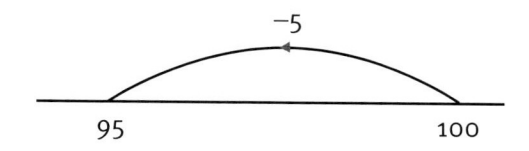

44

Unit 16

Problem 2

Work through the problem in the same way as the first one.

Again, put up two ways of recording it and talk through each one using the empty number line to model solution strategies:

$8 + \square = 60$

$60 - 8 = \square$

The numbers in this case should make it clear that it is easier to subtract rather than count on. But you still might like to model both methods on the empty number line.

Also model on the number line how the five could be split to make the jump back from 60 in two steps.

Linking up the problems

Ask the children to look at both problems and discuss with a partner what they have in common.

Apart from being about superheroes, the children should be able to notice that they are both 'compare' situations. Talk about how both situations involved two amounts that needed to be compared to see which was bigger and by how much. Explain to the children that they are going to be making up some more problems like this.

Follow up

Pairs

Give out problem sheet A. Have sheet B in a prominent place for the children to collect later on.

As the children are working, encourage them to write down whatever mathematical sentences they think are appropriate.

As they finish, ask them to go and collect a copy of sheet B.

Wrap up

Whole class

Invite one or two children to come and show the others the answer to one of the problems from sheet B. Can the class suggest what the problem might have been?

Objectives
- Understand addition problems involving increasing a set
- Model addition using a number line

Big Book problems

This unit returns to addition situations. Previously the children have worked on situations that result in addition from the combining of two separate sets. Here the additions are the result of slightly different types of contexts: a single set is changed and made larger. So we are given the initial quantity, the size of the change and the final resultant size set has to be found.

Whole class

Problem 1

Talk about swimming, sunbathing and frogs!

Ask the children to look at the picture. Discuss the picture and draw their attention to the frogs on the lily pad to the right of the picture. By now the children should be familiar with the routine of needing to decide how many things there are without counting them all. Ask how many frogs there are on the lily pad. Take suggestions, and talk to the children about how they counted. Did anybody see there were five and five?

Ask them to turn to their partner again and to see if they can figure out how many frogs ended up in the water. Although adding on 10 should be quick for many of the children, some children are likely to want to count on in ones. Encourage them to use an empty number line to keep track of their working in this case and to make jumps that are bigger than one at a time. Such children might benefit from having a model of the problem set up with base ten materials: put out 76 as seven ten sticks and six units. Adding on 10 simply means adding one more ten stick to make 80 + 6.

As the children are working on the problem, select two or three who are using different solution methods and invite them to come and share their methods with the class.

Set up the appropriate mathematical sentence :

76 + 10 = ☐

Model on an empty number line how to find the answer in two jumps, followed by how to find it in one jump and discuss which is easier to do.

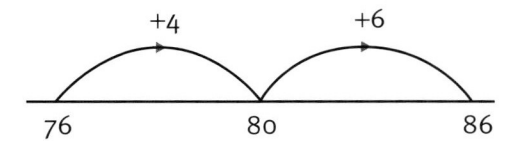

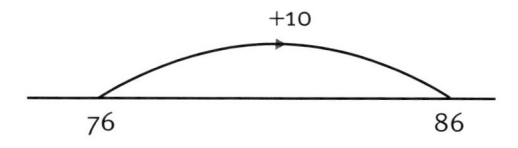

46

Problem 2

Work through the problem in a similar way as the first one. Start by establishing that 49 frogs are sunbathing. Establish that ten more are lined up in the lower right of the picture. Again, some children may benefit from having a model of the problem set up with base ten blocks.

See if anyone can record the mathematical sentence and help them set up on the board:

49 + 10 = ☐

Model how the answer to the question by starting on 49 on the number track and jumping on 10, either in one jump of 10 or two jumps – one of 1 and one of 9.

Linking up the problems

Ask the children to look at both problems and discuss with a partner what they have in common.

Apart from being about frogs, the children should be able to notice that they are both 'add' situations. Talk about how both situations involved an initial number of frogs – 76 in the water, 49 sunbathing – and that this amount was changed or increased in some way – more frogs swimming or sunbathing. Explain to the children that they are going to be solving some more problems like this.

Follow up

Pairs

Give out problem sheet A. Have sheet B in a prominent place for the children to collect later on. As the children are working, encourage them to write down appropriate mathematical sentences. As they finish, ask them to go and collect a copy of sheet B. Explain that they need to work with a friend to complete this sheet.

Wrap up

Whole class

Invite one or two children to come and show the others the problems that they made up and to talk about how they found the answer.

Objectives
- Understand addition problems involving increasing a set
- Model addition using a number line

Big Book problems

This unit builds on the previous one and provides further addition as change situations. Such situations are helpful in encouraging children to use counting on strategies and larger numbers are used here to further encourage this. A number line is used to model counting on strategies.

Whole class

Problem 1

Read through the first problem with the children – repeat it and encourage them to join in.

Ask children to work with a partner to see if they can figure out how many people ended up dancing. Start by establishing that there are 50 people dancing to begin with. Although adding on 30 should be simple for many of the children, some children are likely to want to count on in ones. Encourage them to use an empty number line to keep track of their working in this case and to make jumps that are bigger than one at a time. Such children might benefit from having a model of the problem set up with base ten materials: put out 50 as five ten sticks. Adding on 30 simply means adding three more ten sticks to make 80.

As the children are working on the problem, select who you are going to invite to come and share their methods with the class.

Set up the appropriate mathematical sentence :

$50 + 30 = \square$

Model on an empty number line how to find the answer in jumpsof 10.

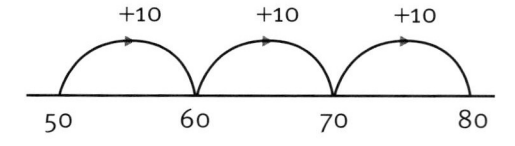

```
    +10      +10      +10
  ⌢        ⌢        ⌢
──┼────────┼────────┼────────┼──
  50       60       70       80
```

48

Unit 18

Problem 2

Work through the problem in a similar way as the first one. Start by establishing that there are 20 people dancing to begin with.

The structure of the problem means that it is likely that some children will want to start with 20 and add on 60. Look out for those who realise that they can start with 60 and add on 20 and choose someone from this group to come and explain their method. Also look out for children who appear to realise that they can use the answer to the first problem to find the answer to this one. Here again, some children may benefit from seeing the situation modeled with base ten blocks.

Set up with the children the two mathematical sentences :

20 + 60 = ☐

60 + 20 = ☐

Does it make any difference which order the numbers are added in?

Model each on an empty number line.

Direct the children's attention to 60 + 20. Can anyone explain why the answer to this is the same as the answer to the first problem, 50 + 30?

Linking up the problems

Ask the children to look at both problems and discuss with a partner what they have in common.

Apart from being about dancing, the children should be able to notice that they are both 'add' situations. Talk about how both situations involved an initial number and that this amount was changed or increased in some way. Explain to the children that they are going to be solving some more problems like this.

Follow up

Pairs

Give out problem sheet A. Have sheet B in a prominent place for the children to collect later on. As the children are working, encourage them to write down appropriate mathematical sentences. As they finish, ask them to go and collect a copy of sheet B. Explain that they need to work with a friend to complete this sheet.

Wrap up

Whole class

Make up one or two similar problems to pose orally to the class. Who can explain how they figured out the answer?

Objectives
- Understand subtraction problems involving taking away
- Model subtraction on a number line

Big Book problems

The two problems here are both subtraction problems. The subtractions are the result of 'change' situations: an initial quantity is changed by something being removed. This is the popular interpretation of subtraction as taking away. These problems link to addition as change problems, but here the change is a decrease rather than an increase. The aim of the lesson is to begin to develop children's ability to recognise subtraction problems and to talk about them as 'change' or 'take away' problems.

Whole class

Problem 1

Talk about Drake the dancer. Has anyone ever heard of Swan Lake or Sleeping Beauty?

Ask the children to look at the picture. Discuss the picture and draw their attention to the ducks in the upper right-hand corner. By now the children should be familiar with the routine of how they need to decide how many items there are, but without counting them all. Ask how many ducks there are. Take suggestions for how many, and talk to the children about how they counted. Did anybody see there were five and five?

Go over the problem with the children. Ask them to turn to a partner and to see if they can figure out how many ducks stay to watch Drake. Although subtracting 10 should be quick for many of the children, some children are likely to want to count back in ones. Encourage them to use an empty number line to keep track of their working in this case and to make jumps that are bigger than one at a time. Such children might benefit from having a model of the problem set up with base ten materials: put out 58 as five ten sticks and eight units. Subtracting 10 simply means removing one ten stick to leave 48.

As the children are working on the problem, select two or three who are using different solution methods and invite them to come and share their methods with the class.

Set up the appropriate mathematical sentence :

$$58 - 10 = \Box$$

Model on an empty number line how to find the answer in two jumps, followed by how to in one jump and discuss which is easier to do.

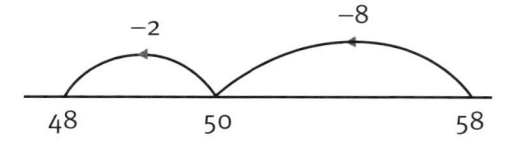

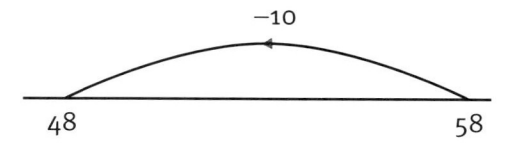

Unit 19

Problem 2

Work through the problem in a similar way as the first one. Start by establishing that 67 moorhens are watching Serena. Establish that ten more are lined up in and walking away in the picture. Again, some children may benefit from having a model of the problem set up with base ten blocks.

See if anyone can record the mathematical sentence and help them set up on the board:

$$67 - 10 = \Box$$

Model how the answer to the question by starting on 67 on the number track and jumping back 10, either in one jump of 10 or two jumps – one of 1 and one of 9. Which do the children think is easier?

Linking up the problems

Ask the children to look at both problems and discuss with a partner what they have in common. Apart from being about birds, the children should be able to notice that they are both 'take away' situations. Talk about how both situations involved an initial number of birds – 58 ducks, 67 moorhens – and that this amount was changed or decreased in some way – 10 ducks or 10 moorhens leaving. Explain to the children that they are going to be solving some more problems like this.

Follow up

Pairs

Give out problem sheet A. Have sheet B in a prominent place for the children to collect later on.

As the children are working, encourage them to write down whatever mathematical sentences they think are appropriate.

As they finish, ask them to go and collect a copy of sheet B.

Wrap up

Whole class

Who spotted which question was the 'odd one out'? How did they know?

Objectives
- Understand subtraction problems involving taking away
- Model subtraction on a number line

Big Book problems

The two problems here are again both subtraction problems. The aim of the lesson is to begin to develop children's ability to recognise subtraction problems and to talk about them as 'change' or 'take away' problems.

Whole class

Problem 1

Talk about the context for the problem. In what ways is this similar to Snow White? In what ways is it different?

Ask the children to look at the picture. Discuss the picture and draw their attention to the cakes in the baking trays. By now, the children should be familiar with the routine of how they need to decide how many things are in the picture, but without counting them all. Ask how many cakes there are in one baking tray. Take suggestions for how many, and talk to the children about how they counted. Did anybody see there were two rows of five?

Next, ask the children to look at the trays of cakes and say how many trays there are. How many cakes is that altogether?

Go over the problem with the children. Make sure that everyone is clear that the giants have eaten 40 cakes from the 70 and that the children have to figure out how many cakes remain (try to avoid explicitly using the language of 'take away').

Some children may know how to record this in a mathematical sentence. Help them record it using the subtraction symbol:

$70 - 40 = \square$

Leave this on the board to refer to later.

Model the solution by counting back in tens on an empty number line.

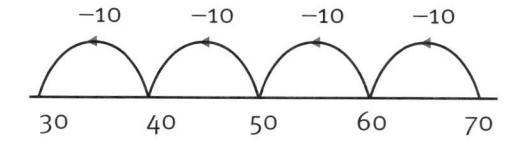

52

Unit 20

Problem 2

Work through the problem in the same way as the first one. As in the first problem, use the 'brief look' approach twice to establish that there are 10 biscuits in each tray and then that there are 8 trays, so that's 80 biscuits.

Again, it might help to model the problem using illustrations for any children having difficulty.

Once one or two children have shared their methods and answers, work with them on recording the appropriate subtraction sentence:

$80 - 40 = \square$

Draw the children's attention back to the sentence 70 – 40. Can anyone see a connection or pattern between the two sentences? Did anyone use the answer to the first problem to find the answer to the second one?

Model finding the answer by counting back on the empty number line.

Linking up the problems

Ask the children to look at both problems and discuss with a partner what they have in common.

Apart from being about hungry giants, the children should be able to notice that they are both 'take away' situations. Talk about how both situations involved starting amounts that were changed by something being removed or taken away. Explain to the children that they are going to be solving some more problems like this.

Follow up

Pairs

Give out problem sheet A. Have sheet B in a prominent place for the children to collect later on.

As the children are working, encourage them to write down whatever mathematical sentences they think are appropriate.

As they finish, ask them to go and collect a copy of sheet B. They need a friend to help.

Wrap up

Whole class

Invite one or two children to come and tell the others the answer to one of the problems that they made up. Can the class come up with suggestions for what the problem might have been?

Objectives
- Understand repeated addition problems
- Model repeated addition on a number line

Big Book problems

This unit and the one that follows, begin, in a simple way to explore multiplication and division. Multiplication is introduced here through a context requiring repeated addition and in the next unit children meet multiplication as arrays.

Whole class

Problem 1

Talk about the context for the problem. What kind of creatures are the Rowdies?

Go over the problem with the children. You might want to model the situation using counters or cubes; this has to be done in such a way as to discourage children from counting all the objects and to encourage them, if they can, to work with mental images. So you might use yogurt cartons as 'buckets' and count 4 'sandwiches' (counters) in each. These then need to positioned so that the children cannot look down into them and count the total number of counters. The children have to figure out how many 'sandwiches' that there are altogether.

Although the model of the problem needs to be set up in such a way that the children cannot easily see all the 'sandwiches' when they come to work it out for themselves, do allow those children who need to represent all four sets of four to do so, perhaps by using objects, or making sketches. As usual, select two or three who are using different solution methods and invited them to come and share their methods with the class.

Some children may be unsure over whether this can be recorded using the addition symbol. If they have only previously experienced adding two objects together, then they may think that using two addition symbols in a number sentence is 'against the rules'. Work on setting up the sentence

$$4 + 4 + 4 + 4 = 16$$

If appropriate, model this as four jumps of four on an empty number line.

Explain to the children that there is another way of recording this situation:

$$4 \times 4 = 16$$ (read as 'four multiplied by four equals nine')

Problem 2

Work through the problem in the same way as the first one. Again, set up the situation with physical objects that are hidden from view once set out.

Unit 21

Once one or two children have shared their methods and answers, work with them on recording the appropriate subtraction sentence:

$$10 + 10 + 10 = 30$$

Again, if appropriate, model this as three jumps of 10 on an empty number line.

Set up the multiplicative way of recording this:

$$10 \times 3 = 15 \text{ (read as 'ten multiplied by three equals thirty')}$$

Linking up the problems

Ask the children to look at both problems and discuss with a partner what they have in common.

Apart from being about the Rowdies' party, they should be able to notice that they are both 'add' situations where several things are added. Explain to the children that they are going to be solving some more problems like this.

Follow up

Pairs

Give out problem sheet A. Have sheet B in a prominent place for the children to collect later on. As the children are working, encourage them to write down whatever mathematical sentences they think are appropriate.

As they finish, ask them to go and collect a copy of sheet B. It is likely that they will need an adult helper to explain questions 2 and 3. For question 2, the children need to be clear that, each time, Father Goose has 12 stones, but a different number of boxes. In question 3, the children have to find ways of putting 24 feathers in bags so that there are an equal number of feathers in each bag (for example 2 bags with 12 in each or 3 bags with 8 in each). They are likely to need objects to help them here.

Wrap up

Whole class

Invite one or two children to come and share with the others two pieces of information from one of their problems from sheet B: the number of containers (for example 6 buckets) and the total number of objects (60 slime sandwiches). Can anyone figure out, in this case, how many slime sandwiches there were in each bucket?

Objectives
- Understand multiplication problems
- Model repeated addition as an array

Big Book problems

This unit follows on from the previous one in exploring the origins of multiplication. Multiplication is introduced here through a context of arrays, complementing the model of multiplication as repeated addition.

Whole class

Problem 1

Talk about the context for the problem. Does anyone collect stamps or stickers?

Go over the problem with the children. Draw the children's attention to the covered up picture. Explain that at the top of the picture there is a 'block' of stamps. Tell the children that they are going to have to try to figure out how many stamps there are altogether. Tell them to look at the top row of three stamps. Make sure everyone is clear that there are three stamps in this first row and tell them that there are the same number of stamps in each row.

Explain that you are now going to look at how many rows there are. Point to the first column of four stamps. Point to each in turn and emphasize that there are 3 stamps in each row. Ask the children to turn to their neighbour and to figure out how many stamps there are altogether. Take answers from the children and explanations of how they got to their answer.

Invite children to describe the 3×4 array of stamps and encourage statements like:

> It's three across and four down
>
> There are three rows
>
> There are four columns

Set up the multiplication sentence to represent this:

$3 \times 4 = 12$

Leave this on the board.

Direct the children's attention to the first picture of chewed up stamps. Make sure that the children are clear that before Max chewed some, this was a rectangular array of stamps. Working with a partner, can they figure out how many stamps were there before Max got at them?

Unit 22

Explore with the children how they know that there must have been 12. Can anyone come and write the multiplication sentence to go with this array?

$6 \times 2 = 12$

Problem 2

Work through the second chewed array in the same way as the first one. This time, some children may need to sketch out the complete array in order to find the solution. Do not discourage them from doing so. Children who are having difficulty might be advised to try and sketch the complete array.

Once one or two children have shared their methods and answers, work with them on recording the appropriate subtraction sentence:

$5 \times 4 = 20$

Linking up the problems

Ask the children to look at both problems and discuss with a partner what they have in common.

Apart from being about stamps, the children should be able to notice that they are both 'add' situations where three things are added. Explain to the children that they are going to be solving some more problems like this.

Follow up

Pairs

Give out problem sheet A. Have sheet B in a prominent place for the children to collect later on. As the children are working, encourage them to write down whatever mathematical sentences they think are appropriate.

As they finish, ask them to go and collect a copy of sheet B. It is likely that they will need an adult helper to explain questions 2 and 3. For question 2, the children need to be clear that each time, Mary has 24 silver bells, but puts a different number into each bag. In question 3, the children have to find ways of putting 36 sunflowers in jars so that there are an equal number of sunflowers in each jar (for example, 3 jars with 12 in each or 4 jars with 9 in each). They are likely to need objects to help them here.

Wrap up

Whole class

Hold up some examples of torn grids from sheet B. Who can figure out how many stamps there were in the whole grid. What information did they need to use to figure this out?

Objectives
- Understand division as sharing problems
- Model repeated subtraction with objects or pictures

Big Book problems

This unit introduces, in a simple way, the model of division as sharing. The other model for division is as repeated subtraction which they meet in the next unit.

Whole class

Problem 1

Talk about the context for the problem. Does anyone know the story of Mother Goose?

Read through the first problem with the children. Check that everyone is clear that Mother Goose has 12 eggs and 3 baskets and she is putting the same number of eggs into each basket. Getting some children to explain the problem in their own words will help them understand the situation.

When figuring out the answer, children may need to model this situation with counters or cubes.

Go over the problem solution with the children. You might want to model the situation using counters or cubes; counting out 12 and sharing these into bags.

Record the mathematical sentence:

$$12 \div 3 = 4$$

Problem 2

Work through the problem in the same way as the first one.

Once one or two children have shared their methods and answers, work with them on setting up the mathematical sentence:

$$16 \div 4 = 4$$

Unit 23

Linking up the problems

Ask the children to look at both problems and discuss with a partner what they have in common.

Apart from being about Mother and Father Goose, the children should begin to be able to talk about them both being 'sharing' situations. Explain to the children that they are going to be solving some more problems like this.

Follow up

Pairs

Give out problem sheet A. Have sheet B in a prominent place for the children to collect later on.

As the children are working, encourage them to write down whatever mathematical sentences they think are appropriate.

As they finish, ask them to go and collect a copy of sheet B.

Wrap up

Whole class

Take suggestions from the class for different ways of sharing 24 feathers equally. Work on organizing their ideas in an orderly way (2 bags, 3 bags, 4 bags and so on). Have they found all the possible ways?

Objectives
- Understand division as repeated subtraction problems
- Model division with objects or pictures

Big Book problems

This unit introduces the model of division as repeated subtraction. The intention is not that children should begin themselves to use the notation of division to represent repeated subtraction. It is simply that they are exposed to the notation.

Whole class

Problem 1

Talk about the context for the problem. Does anyone remember the nursery rhyme 'Mary, Mary, quite contrary'?

Read through the first problem with the children. Check that everyone is clear that Mary has 18 shells and and she is putting three shells into each basket. Getting some children to explain the problem in their own words will help them understand that they have to figure out how many baskets Mary needs.

When figuring out the answer, children may need to model this situation with counters or cubes.

Go over the problem solution with the children. You might want to model the situation using counters or cubes; counting out 18 and putting these 3 to a bag bags.

Record the mathematical sentence:

$18 \div 3 = 6$

Problem 2

Work through the problem in the same way as the first one.

As the numbers are larger here, have base 10 blocks available for those children who need to work practically.

Once one or two children have shared their methods and answers, work with them on setting up the mathematical sentence:

$60 \div 10 = 6$

Unit 24

Linking up the problems

Ask the children to look at both problems and discuss with a partner what they have in common.

Apart from being about Mary and her shells and bells, the children should begin to be able to talk about them both being 'take away' situations where three things are subtracted each time. Explain to the children that they are going to be solving some more problems like this.

Follow up

Pairs

Give out problem sheet A. Have sheet B in a prominent place for the children to collect later on.

As the children are working, encourage them to write down whatever mathematical sentences they think are appropriate.

As they finish, ask them to go and collect a copy of sheet B.

Wrap up

Whole class

Take suggestions from the class for different ways of sharing 36 sunflowers equally. Work on organizing their ideas in an orderly way (2 jars, 3 jars, 4 jars and so on). Have they found all the possible ways?

Year 1

Unit 1	**Cats and Dogs**
Unit 2	**Big Blue Riding Hood**
Unit 3	**Rastpunzel**
Unit 4	**Mermaid and merman**
Unit 5	**Cinderfella**
Unit 6	**Trainer life**
Unit 7	**Munch time**
Unit 8	**Flatz**
Unit 9	**Hide and Seek**
Unit 10	**Monsters Sink**
Unit 11	**Baldilocks**
Unit 12	**Jill and Jack**

Year 2

Unit 13	**Circus Nights**
Unit 14	**On the Buses**
Unit 15	**The Sprats**
Unit 16	**Invincibles**
Unit 17	**Leaping frogs**
Unit 18	**Knock, knock**
Unit 19	**Sleeping Ugly**
Unit 20	**Sam White**
Unit 21	**Rowdies**
Unit 22	**Naughty Max**
Unit 23	**Mama and Papa Goose**
Unit 24	**Mary, Mary**

Cats and Dogs

Unit 1/A

1. Add some cats to the game.

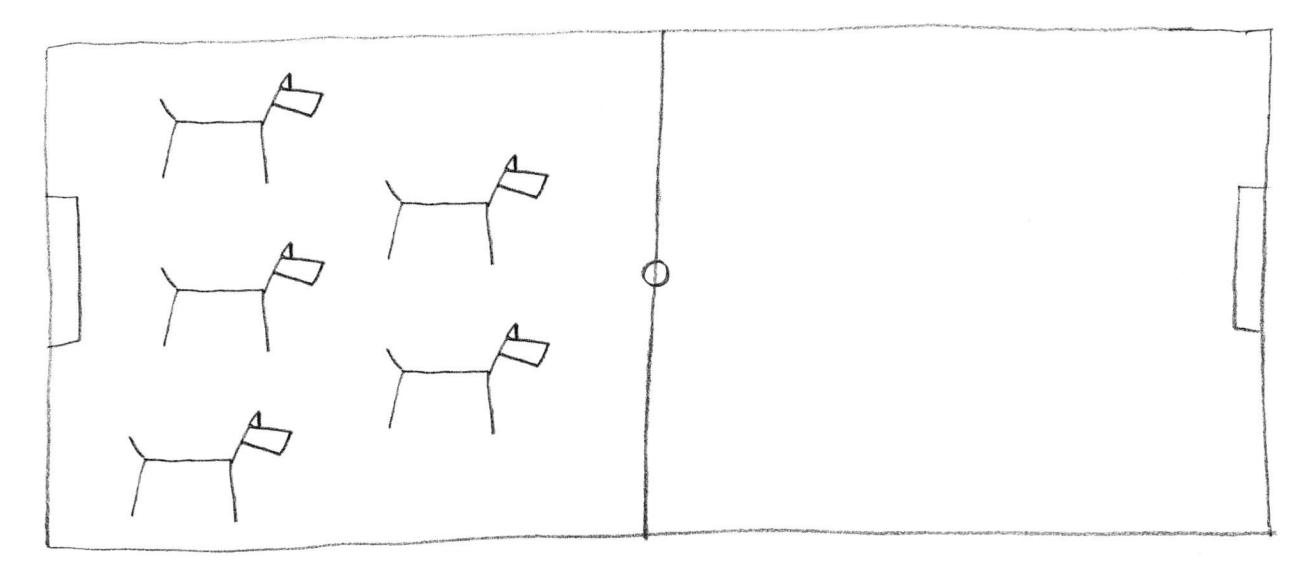

How many cats and dogs are playing?

2. Add some dogs to the game.

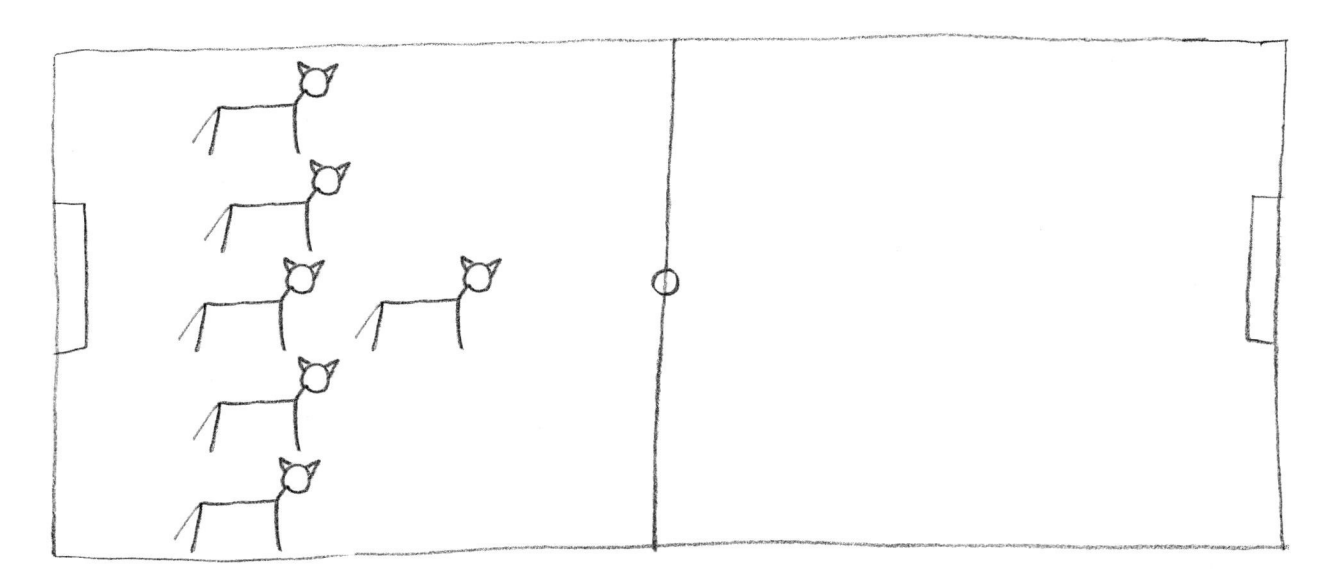

How many cats and dogs are playing?

BEAM's Big Book of Word Problems © BEAM Education

Cats and Dogs

Unit 1/B

1. Draw some dogs. Ask a friend to draw some cats.

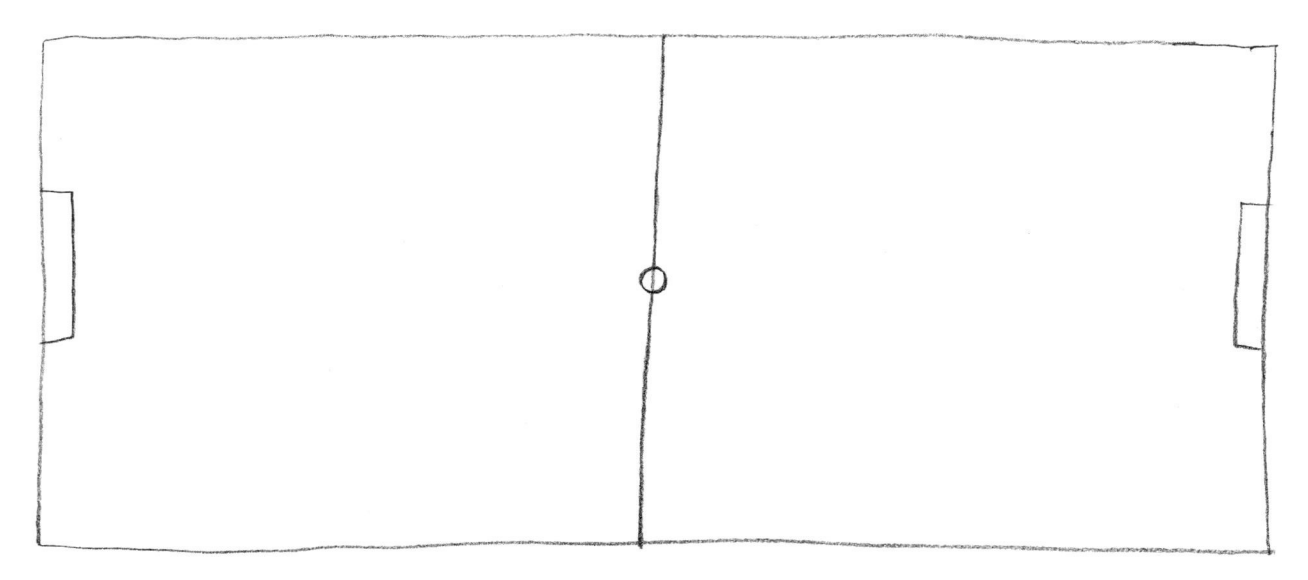

How many cats and dogs are playing?

2. Draw some cats. Ask a friend to draw some dogs.

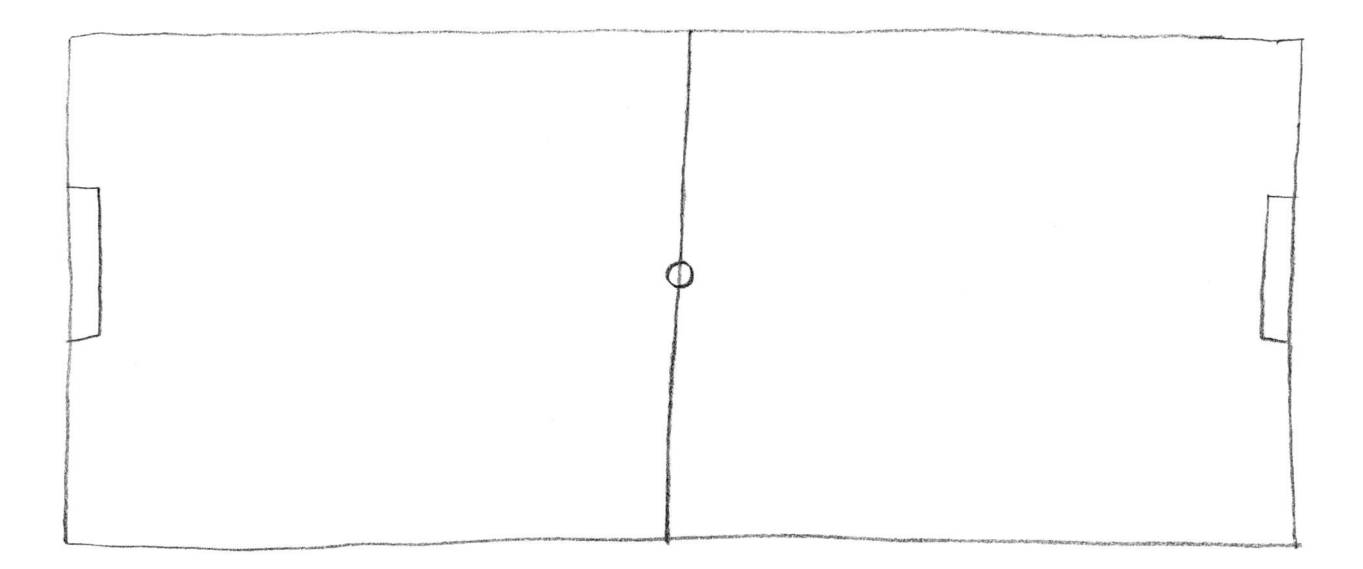

How many cats and dogs are playing?

Big Blue Riding Hood

Unit 2/A

1. Draw some apples in the basket.

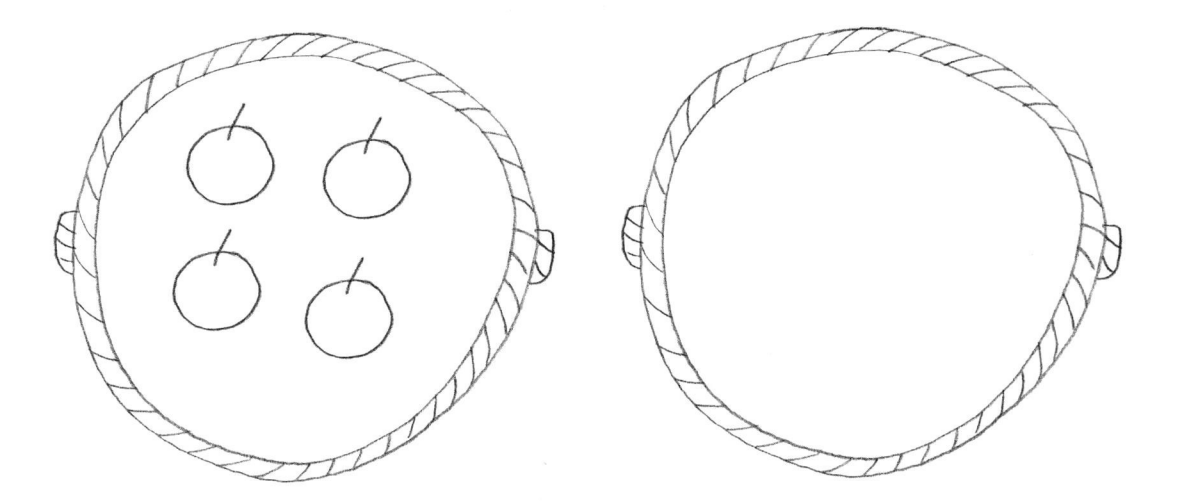

How many apples are in both baskets?

2. Draw some pies in the basket.

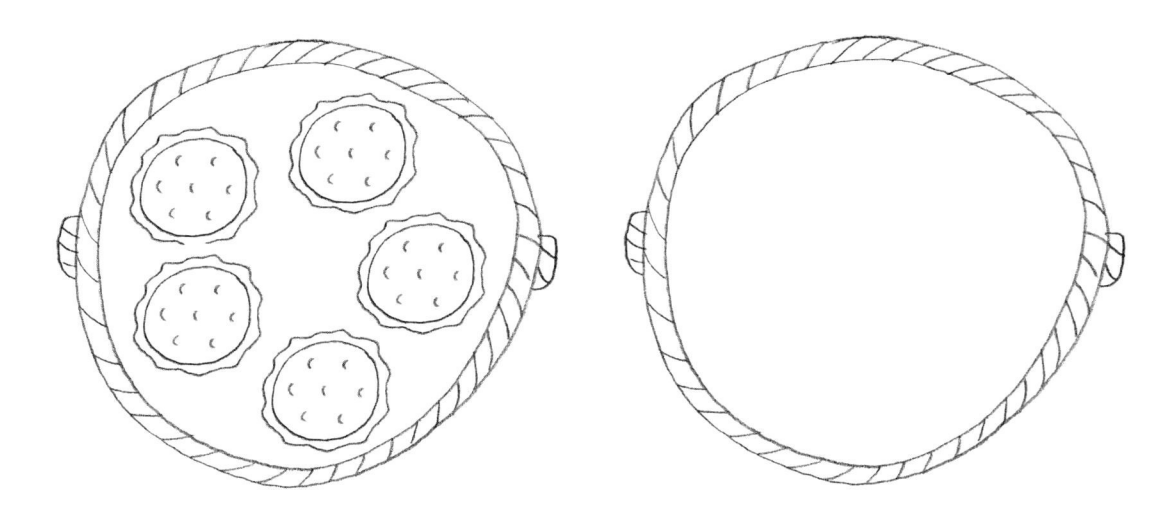

How many pies are in both baskets?

BEAM's Big Book of Word Problems

© BEAM Education

Big Blue Riding Hood

Unit 2/B

1. Draw some apples in the baskets.

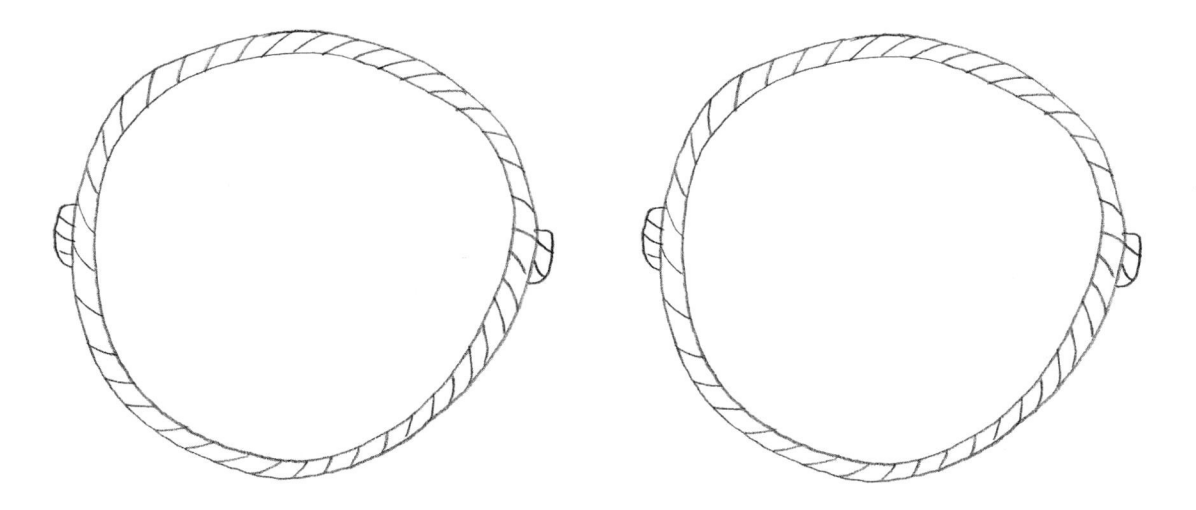

How many apples are in the baskets?

2. Draw some pies in the baskets.

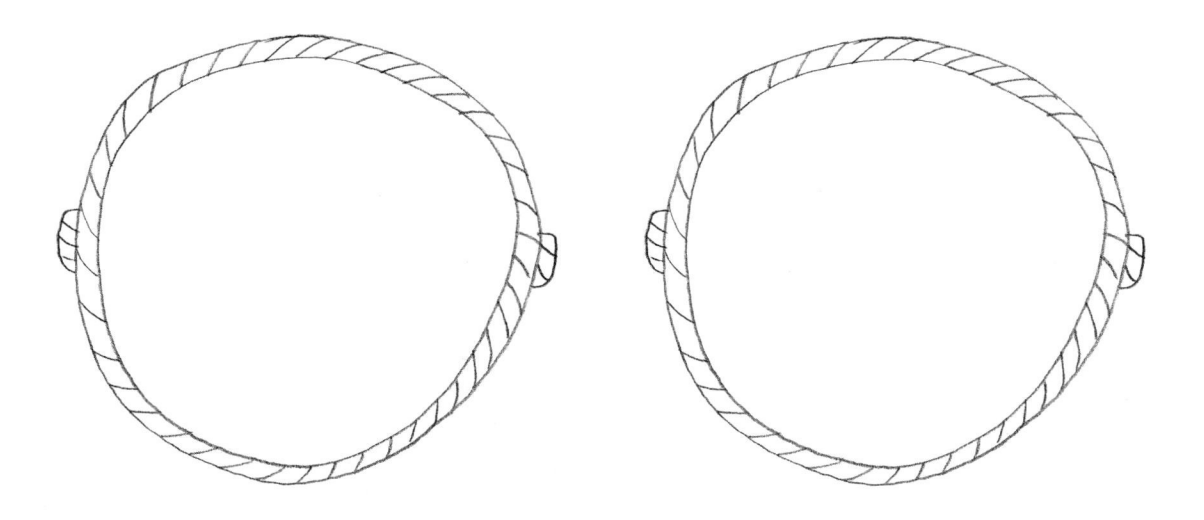

How many pies are in the baskets?

Rastpunzel

Unit 3/A

1. Make the box have 10 combs

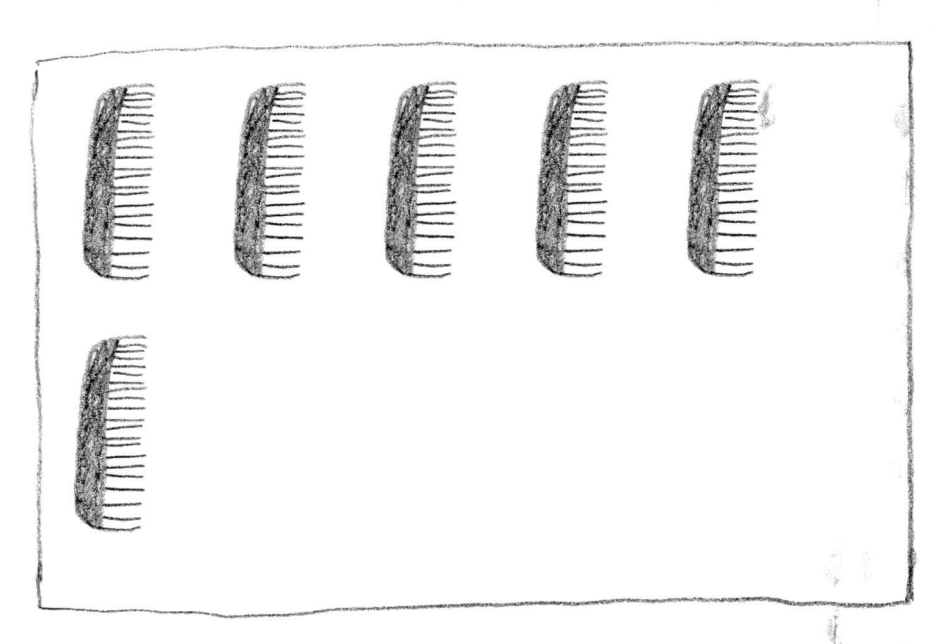

   Record the numbers.

2. Make the box have 10 hats.

   Record the numbers.

BEAM's Big Book of Word Problems © BEAM Education

Rastpunzel

Unit 3/B

1. Draw some combs.

   Ask a friend to make the box have 10 combs.

   Record the numbers.

2. Draw some hats.

   Ask a friend to make the box have 10 hats.

   Record the numbers.

BEAM's Big Book of Word Problems © BEAM Education

Mermaid and merman

Unit 4/A

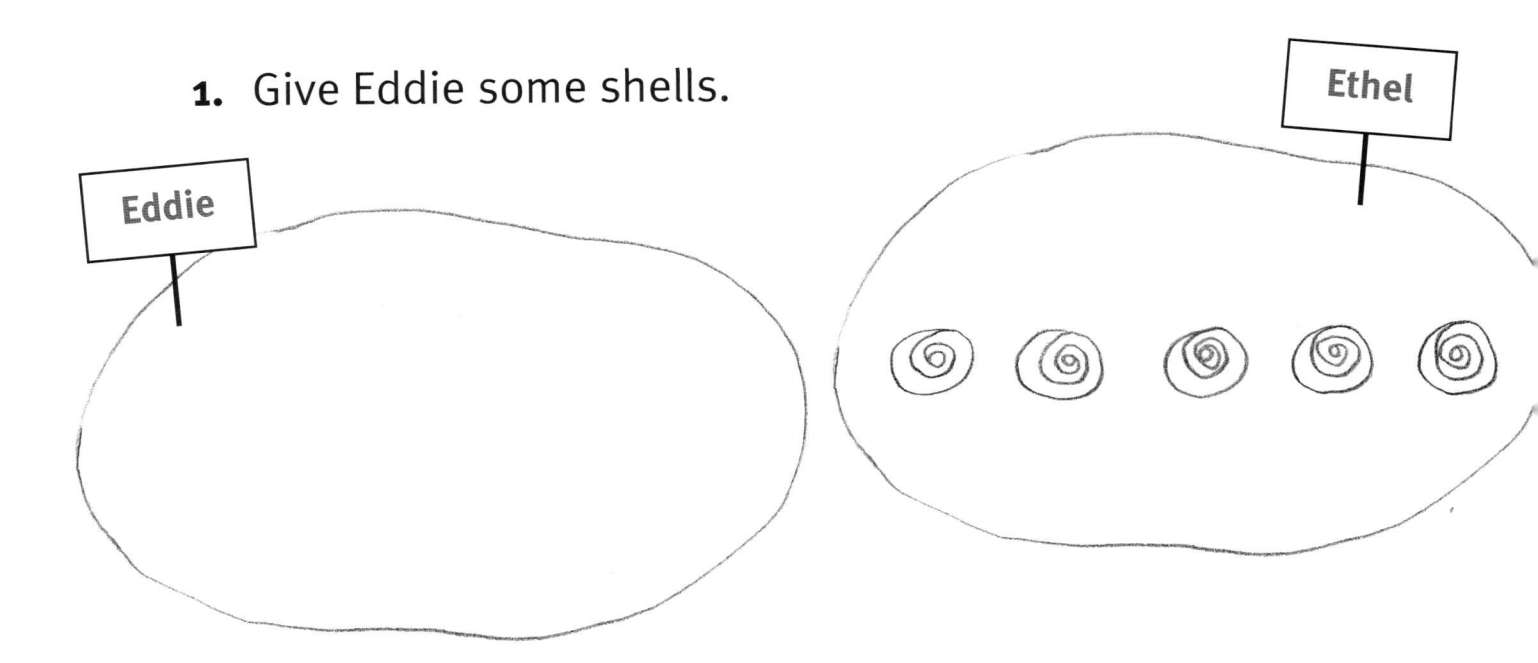

1. Give Eddie some shells.

Eddie

Ethel

Who has more shells?

How many more?

2. Give Ethel some stars.

Eddie

Ethel

Who has more stars?

How many more?

BEAM's Big Book of Word Problems © BEAM Education

Mermaid and merman

Unit 4/B

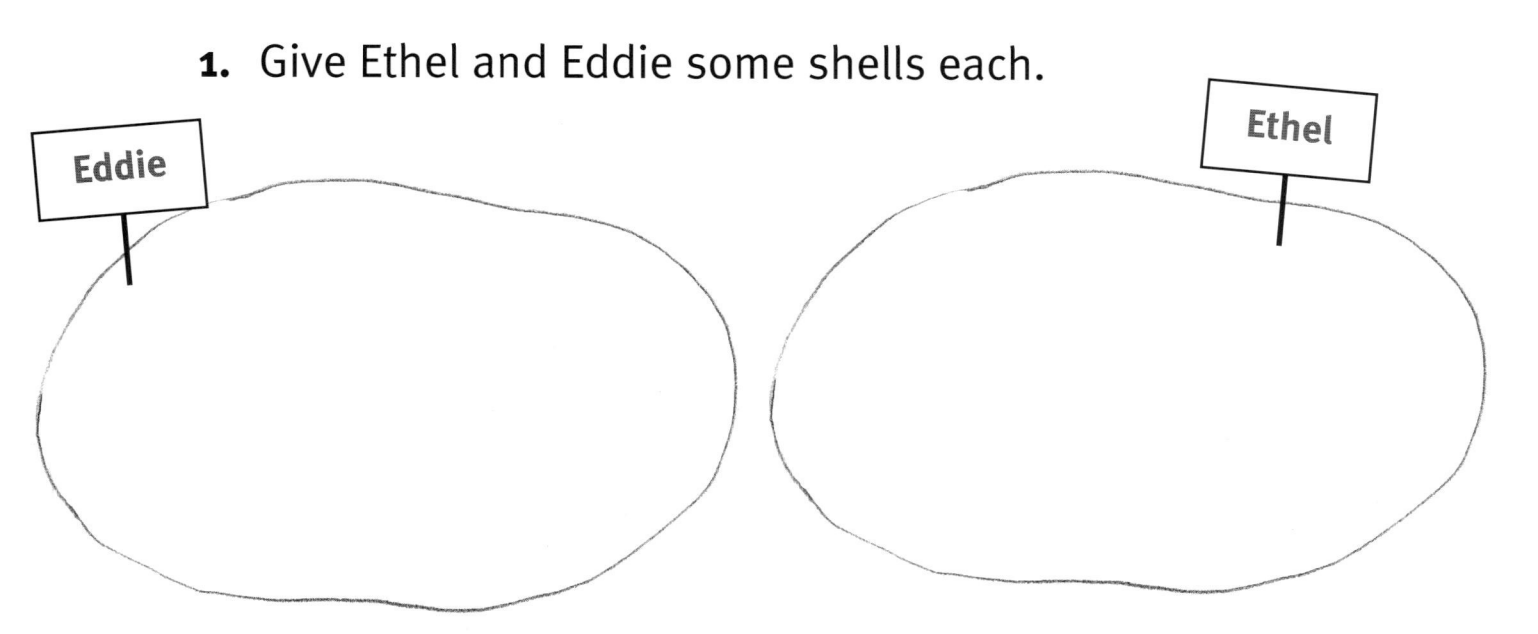

1. Give Ethel and Eddie some shells each.

Eddie

Ethel

Who has more shells?

How many more?

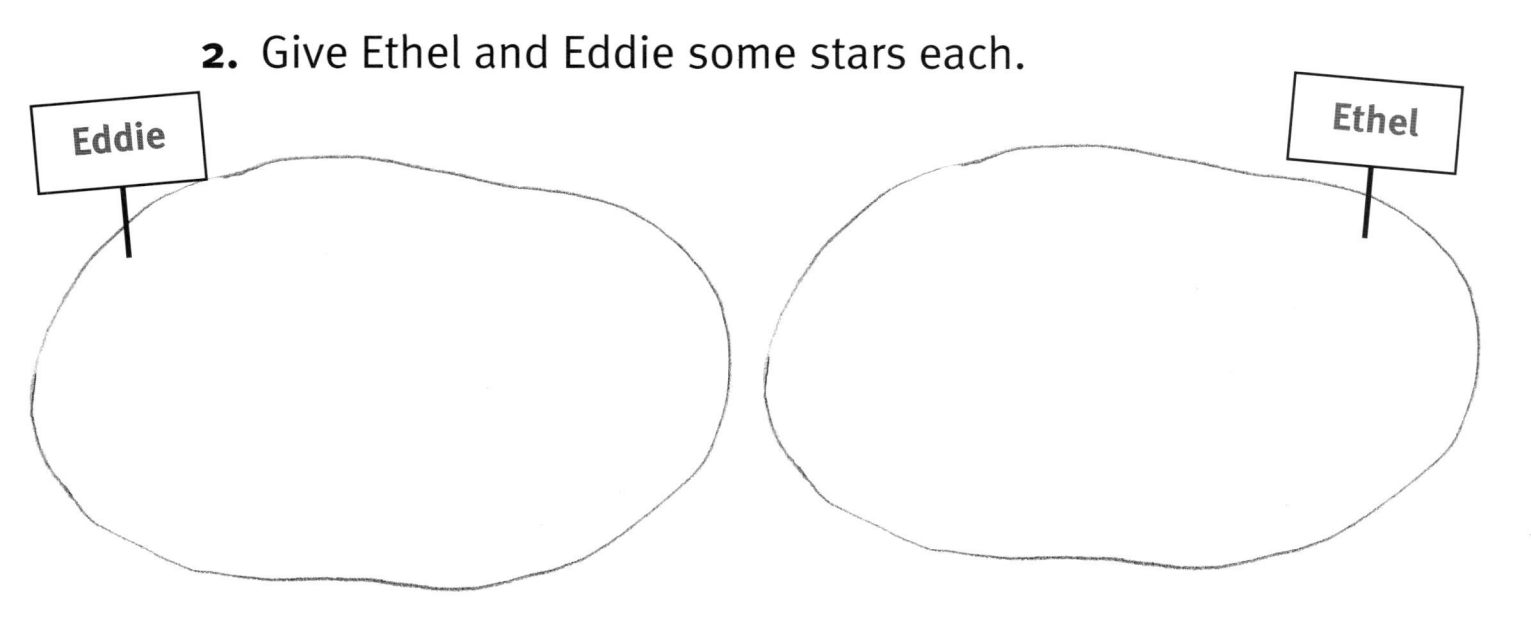

2. Give Ethel and Eddie some stars each.

Eddie

Ethel

Who has more stars?

How many more?

BEAM's Big Book of Word Problems © BEAM Education

Cinderfella

Unit 5/A

1. Give Harry some boots.

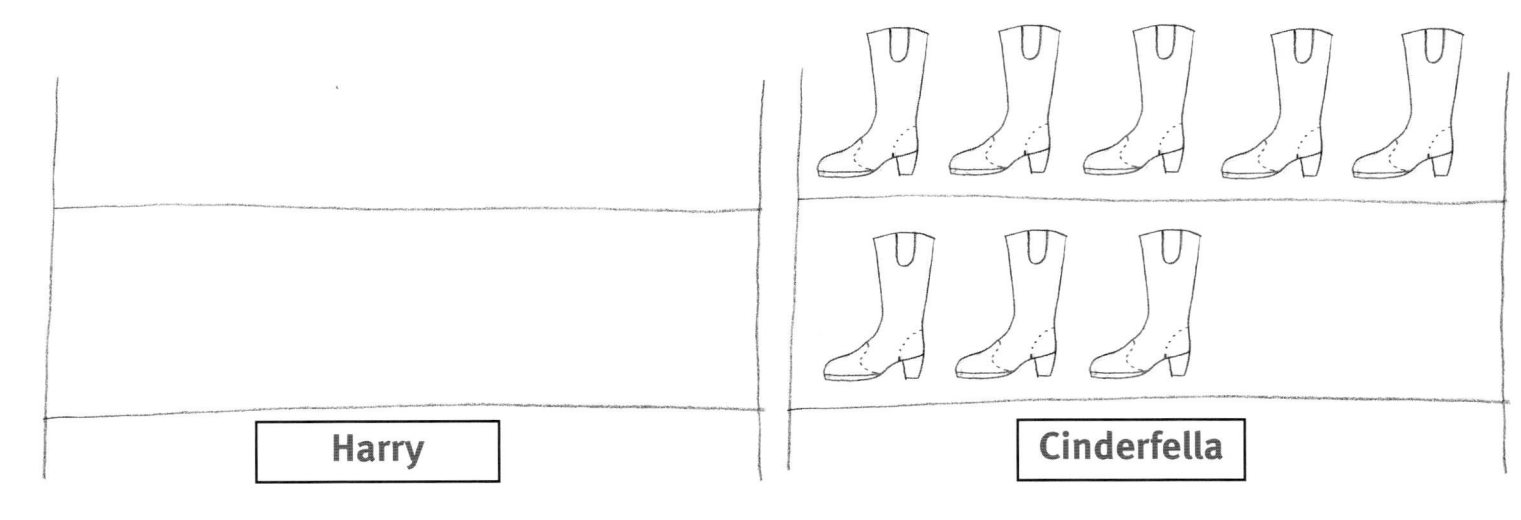

Harry

Cinderfella

Who has more boots?

How many more?

2. Give Will some socks.

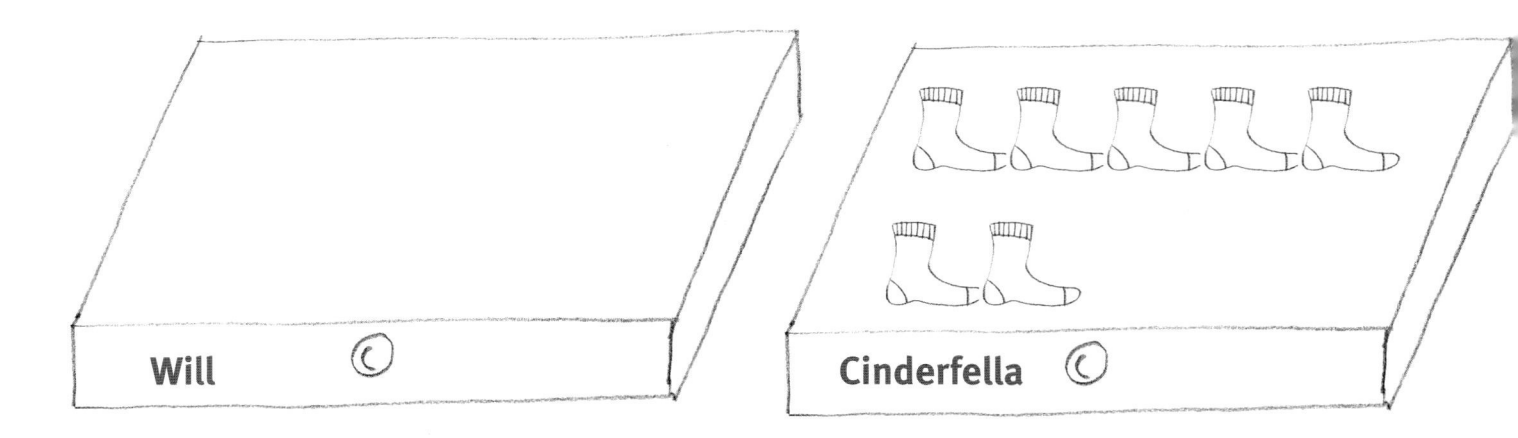

Will

Cinderfella

Who has more socks?

How many more?

Cinderfella

Unit 5/B

1. Give Cinderfella and Harry some boots each.

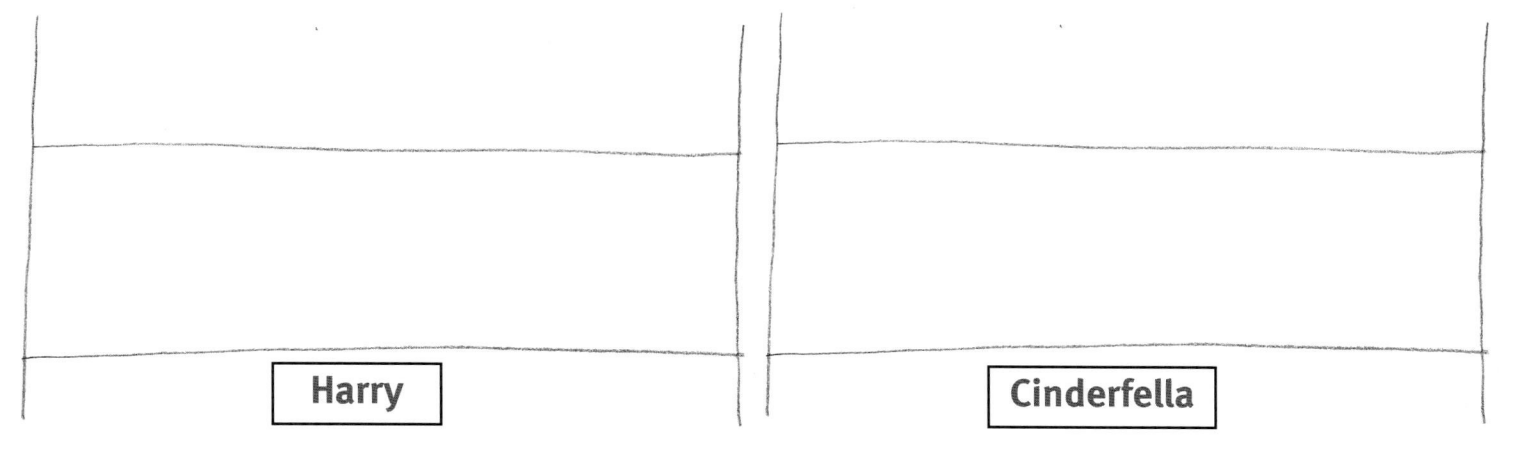

| Harry | Cinderfella |

Who has more boots?

How many more?

2. Give Cinderfella and Will some socks each.

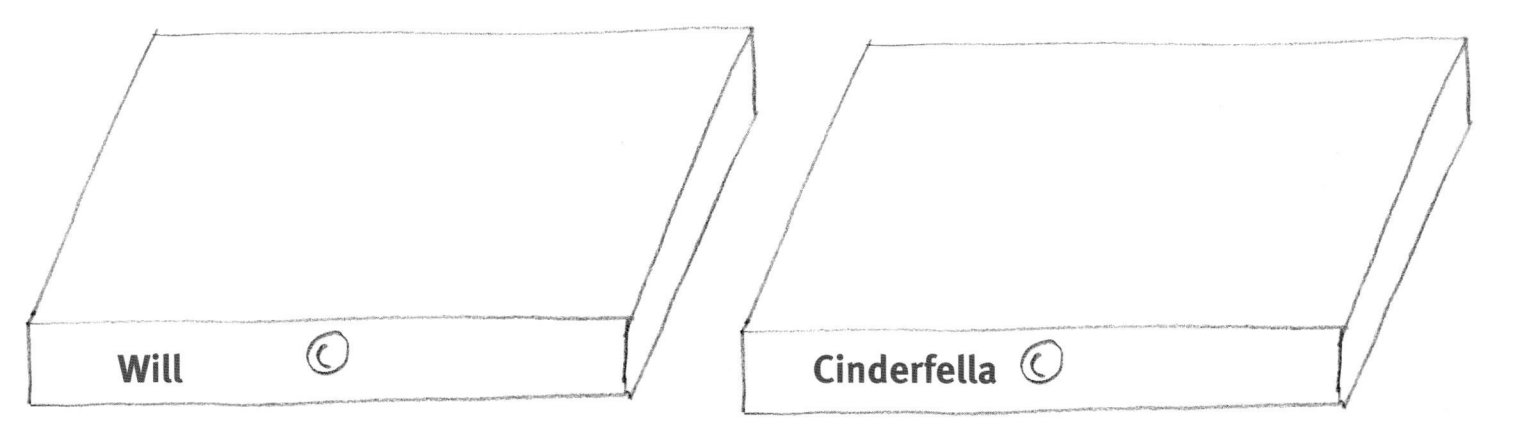

| Will | Cinderfella |

Who has more socks?

How many more?

BEAM's Big Book of Word Problems © BEAM Education

Trainer life

Unit 6/A

1. Put some more mice at the table.

How many mice are having supper?

2. Put some more mice in the bed.

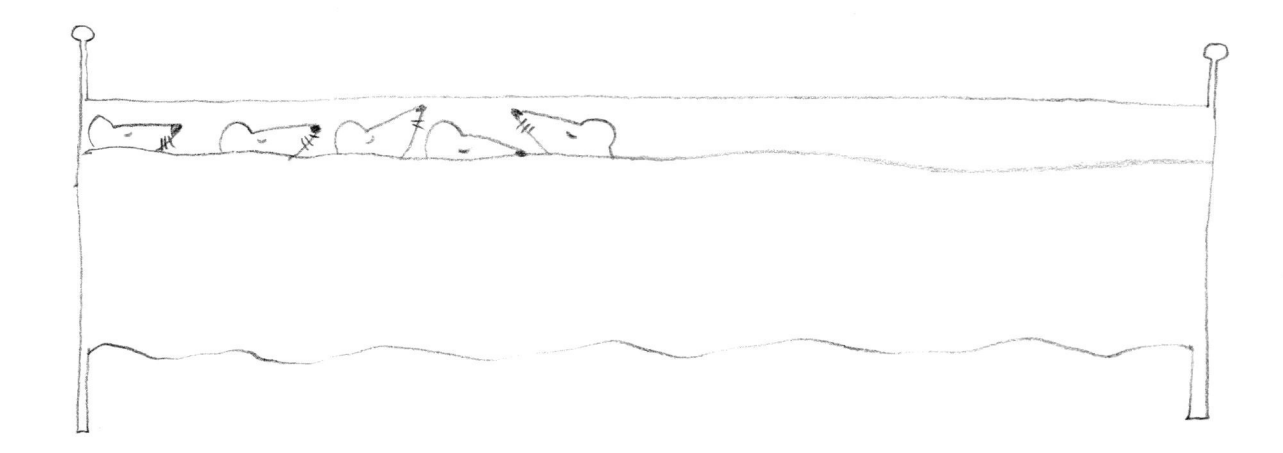

How many mice are in bed?

BEAM's Big Book of Word Problems © BEAM Education

Trainer life

Unit 6/B

1. Put some mice at the table.

Ask a friend to put some more mice at the table.

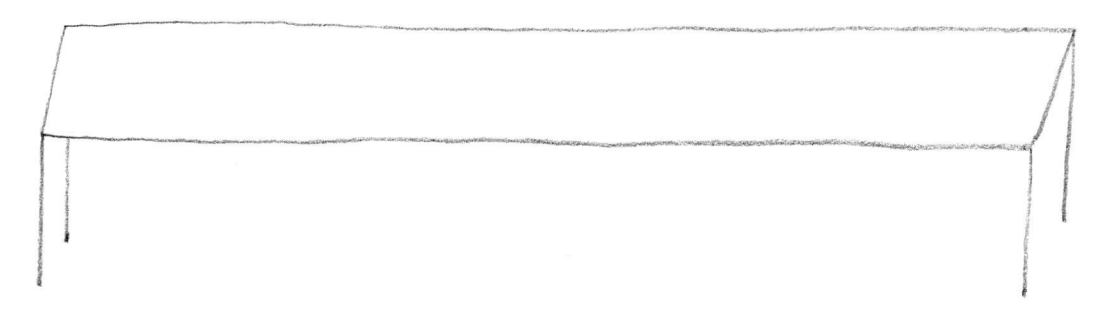

How many mice are having supper?

2. Put some mice in the bed.

Ask a friend to put some more mice in the bed.

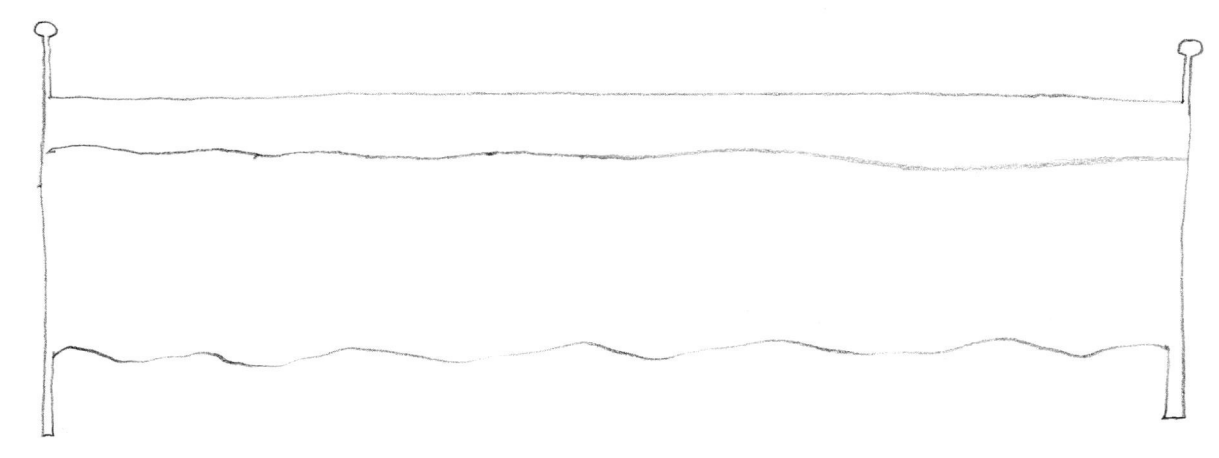

How many mice are in bed?

BEAM's Big Book of Word Problems © BEAM Education

Munch time

Unit 7/A

1. Give Maisie some more apples.

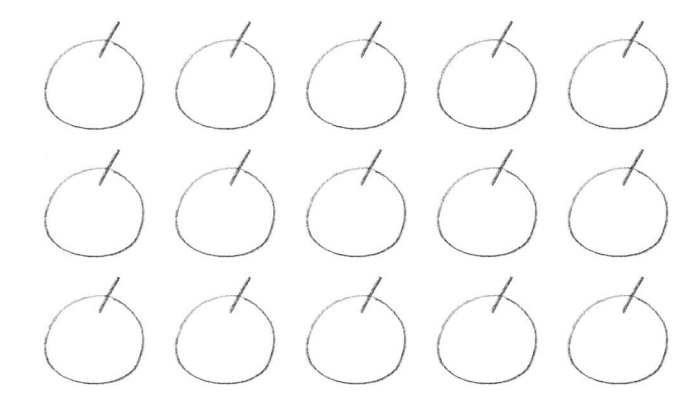

How many apples does Maisie have for tea?

2. Give Maisie some more carrots.

How many carrots does Maisie have for lunch?

Munch time

Unit 7/B

1. Draw some apples for Maisie.

Ask a friend to draw some more apples for Maisie.

How many apples does Maisie have for tea?

2. Draw some carrots for Maisie.

Ask a friend to draw some more carrots for Maisie.

How many carrots does Maisie have for lunch?

Flatz

Unit 8/A

1. Draw some Flatz to make 16 dancing Flatz.

   Record the numbers.

2. Draw some Flatz to make 12 Flatz with ice creams.

   Record the numbers.

Flatz

Unit 8/B

1. Ask a friend to draw some dancing Flatz.

Draw some more to make 17 dancing Flatz.

Record the numbers.

2. Ask a friend to draw some Flatz with ice creams.

Draw some more to make 13 Flatz with ice creams.

Record the numbers.

Hide and Seek

Unit 9/A

1. Hide 3 elephants.

How many elephants are **not** hiding?

Record the numbers.

2. Hide 4 spiders.

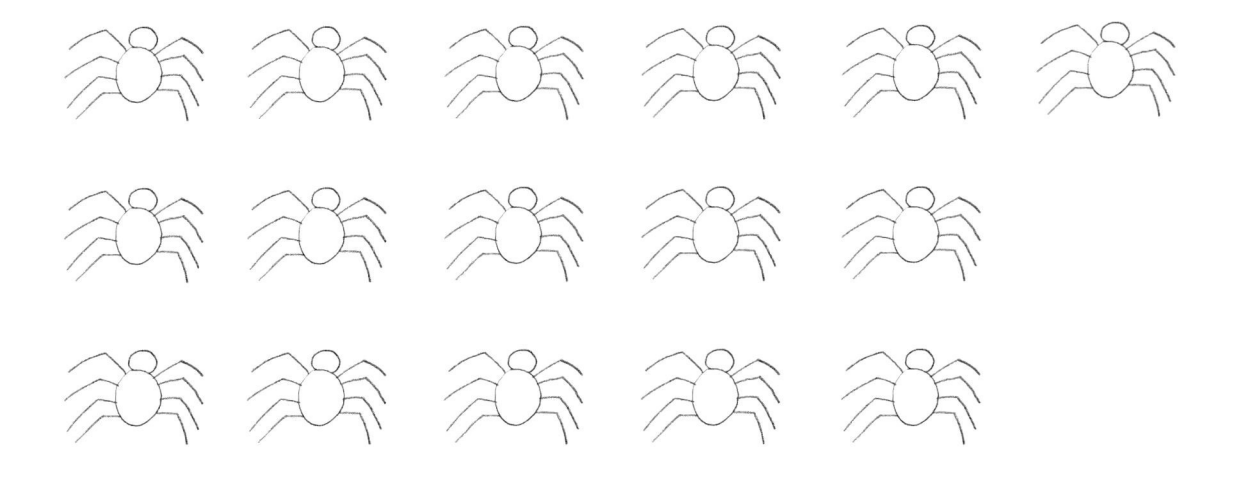

How many spiders are **not** hiding?

Record the numbers.

BEAM's Big Book of Word Problems © BEAM Education

Hide and Seek

Unit 9/B

1. Three elephants are hiding.

How many elephants are there altogether?

Record the numbers.

2. Four spiders are hiding.

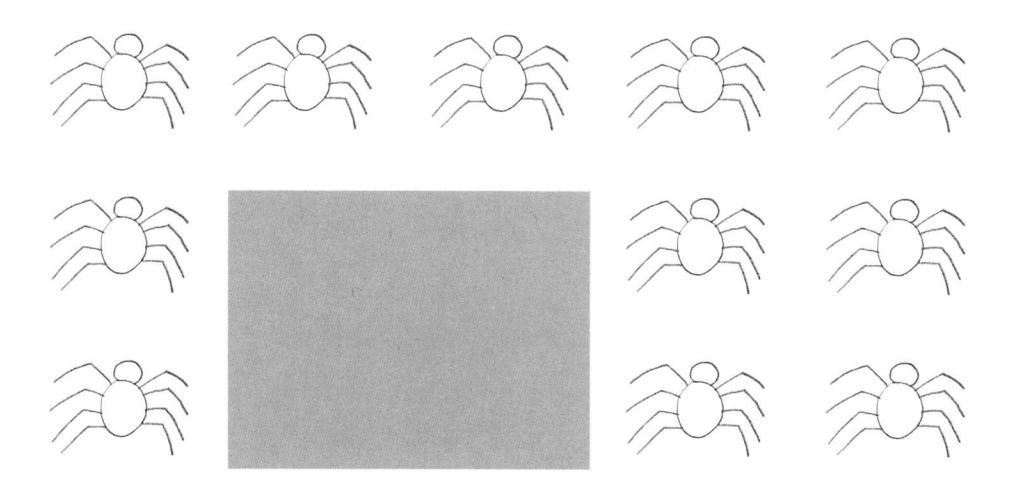

How many spiders are there altogether?

Record the numbers.

Monsters Sink

Unit 10/A

1. Hide 4 earwigs.

   How many earwigs are **not** hiding?

   Record the numbers.

2. Hide 6 eyelashes.

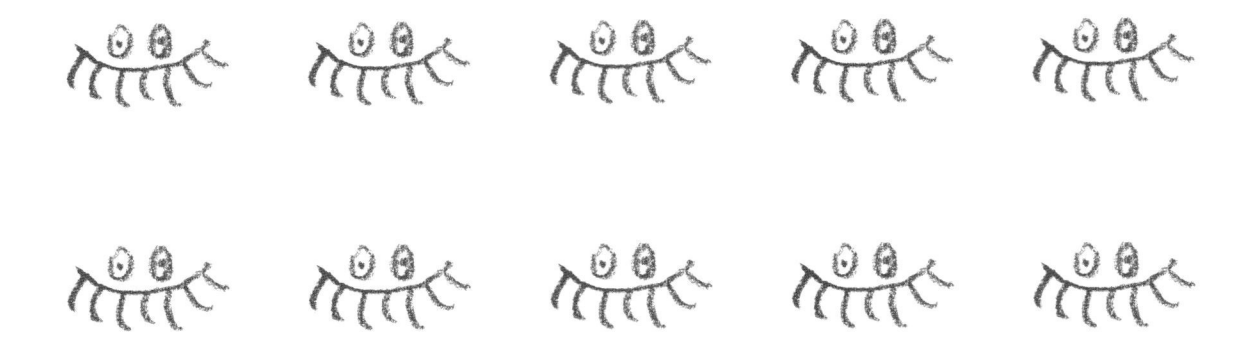

   How many eyelashes are **not** hiding?

   Record the numbers.

BEAM's Big Book of Word Problems © BEAM Education

Monsters Sink

Unit 10/B

1. Three earwigs are hiding.

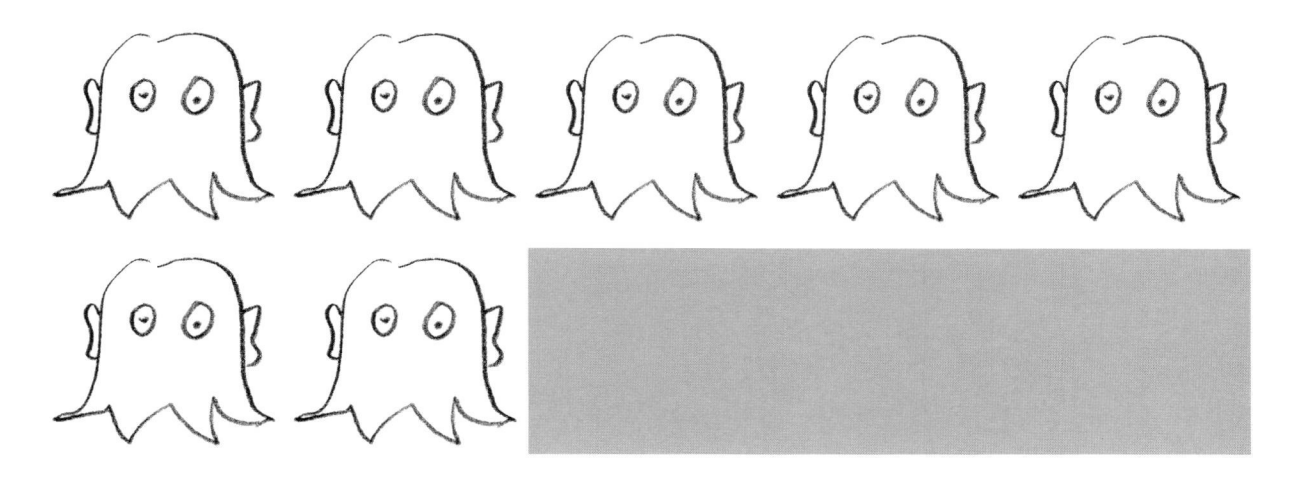

   How many earwigs are there altogether?

   Record the numbers.

2. Five eyelashes are hiding.

   How many eyelashes are there altogether?

   Record the numbers.

Baldilocks

Unit 11/A

1. Draw the same number of cushions on each chair.

   How many cushions are there altogether?

   Record the numbers.

2. Draw the same number of strawberries on each plate.

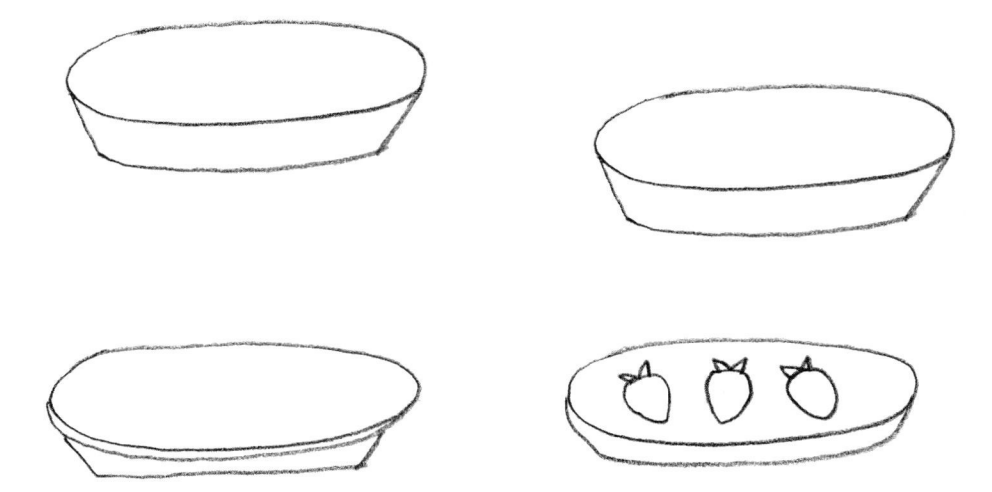

   How many strawberries are there altogether?

   Record the numbers.

BEAM's Big Book of Word Problems © BEAM Education

Baldilocks

Unit 11/B

1. Ask a friend to draw some cushions on one chair.

   Draw the same number of cushions on each chair.

   How many cushions are there altogether?

   Record the numbers.

2. Ask a friend to draw some strawberries on one plate.

   Draw the same number of strawberries on each plate.

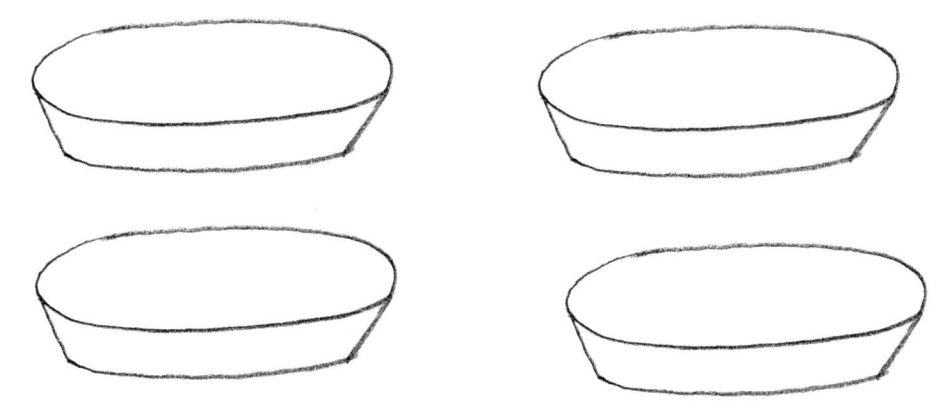

   How many strawberries are there altogether?

   Record the numbers.

Jill and Jack

Unit 12/A

1. Jill has 8 buckets.

Jill puts 4 buckets in each box.

Draw the buckets in the boxes.

2. Jack has 15 bottles.

Jack puts 3 bottles in each box.

Draw the bottles in the boxes.

Jill and Jack

Unit 12/B

1. Jill has 8 buckets.

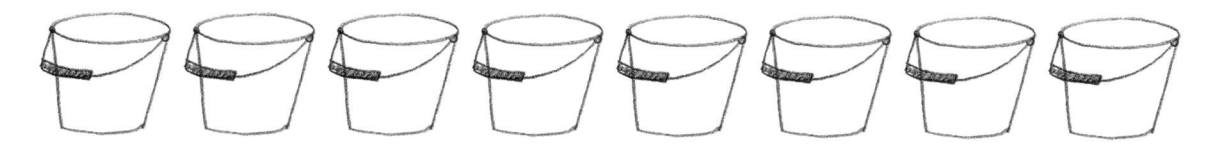

Jill puts the buckets into boxes.
She puts the same number of buckets in each box.

Draw the buckets in the boxes.

1. Jack has 12 bottles.

Jack puts the bottles into boxes.
He puts the same number of bottles in each box.

Draw the bottles in the boxes.

BEAM's Big Book of Word Problems © BEAM Education

Circus Nights

Unit 13/A

1. Jojo can balance on 54 plates.

   Jojo can juggle with 5 plates.

   How many plates does Jojo use to balance on and juggle with?

2. Jemma can balance on 6 cups.

   Jemma can carry 72 cups.

   How many cups does Jemma use to balance on and carry?

3. Jojo can balance on 5 bowls.

   Jojo can carry 45 bowls.

   How many bowls does Jojo use to balance on and carry?

Circus Nights

Unit 13/B

Ask a friend to fill in the missing numbers.

1. Jojo can balance on 54 plates.

    Jojo can juggle with ☐ plates.

    How many plates does Jojo use to balance on and juggle with?

2. Jemma can balance on 6 cups.

    Jemma can juggle with ☐ cups.

    How many cups does Jemma use to balance on and carry?

3. Jojo can balance on ☐ bowls.

    Jojo can carry 45 bowls.

    How many bowls does Jojo use to balance on and carry?

BEAM's Big Book of Word Problems © BEAM Education

On the Buses

Unit 14/A

1. The 68 bus is busy.

   60 people are downstairs on the bus.

   8 people are upstairs on the bus.

   How many people are on the busy 68 bus?

2. The 79 bus is busy.

   8 people are upstairs on the bus.

   70 people are downstairs on the bus.

   How many people are on the busy 79 bus?

3. The 18 bus is busy.

   25 people are upstairs on the bus.

   75 people are downstairs on the bus.

   How many people are on the busy 18 bus?

On the Buses

Unit 14/B

Ask a friend to fill in the missing numbers.

1. The 25 bus is busy.

    40 people are downstairs on the bus.

    ☐ people are upstairs on the bus.

    How many people are on the busy 25 bus?

2. The 43 bus is busy.

    7 people are upstairs on the bus.

    ☐ people are downstairs on the bus.

    How many people are on the busy 43 bus?

3. The D8 bus is busy.

    ☐ people are upstairs on the bus.

    ☐ people are downstairs on the bus.

    How many people are on the busy D8 bus?

The Sprats

Unit 15/A

1. Jack Sprat can eat 68 grapes.

   Jill Sprat can only eat 6 grapes.

   How many more grapes can Jack eat than Jill can?

2. Jill Sprat can eat 98 nuts.

   Jack Sprat can only eat 7 nuts.

   How many more nuts can Jill eat than Jack can?

3. Jill Sprat can eat 5 peas.

   Jack Sprat can eat 48 peas.

   How many more peas can Jack eat than Jill can?

The Sprats

Unit 15/B

Ask a friend to fill in the missing numbers.

1. Jack Sprat can eat 57 grapes.

   Jill Sprat does not like grapes.

   Jill Sprat can only eat ☐ grapes.

   How many more grapes can Jack eat than Jill can?

2. Jill Sprat can eat 79 nuts.

   Jack Sprat does not like nuts.

   Jack Sprat can only eat ☐ nuts.

   How many more nuts can Jill eat than Jack can?

3. Jill Sprat can eat 4 peas.

   Jack Sprat likes peas.

   Jack Sprat can eat ☐ peas.

   How many more peas can Jack eat than Jill can?

Invincibles

Unit 16/A

1. Steph Stretch can carry 80 hamsters.

Norma Normal can carry 6 hamsters.

How many more hamsters can Steph carry than Norma can?

2. Max Maxi can carry 40 books.

Norm Normal can carry 5 books.

How many more books can Max carry than Norm can?

3. Norm Normal can carry 4 bags.

Steph Stretch can carry 70 bags.

How many more bags can Steph carry than Norm can?

Invincibles

Unit 16/B

Ask a friend to fill in the missing numbers.

1. Steph Stretch can carry 80 hamsters.

   Norma Normal cannot carry many hamsters.

   Norma Normal can carry ☐ hamsters.

   How many more Hamsters can Steph carry than Norma can?

2. Max Maxi can carry 30 books.

   Norm Normal cannot carry many books.

   Norm Normal can carry ☐ books.

   How many more books can Max carry than Norm can?

3. Norma Normal can carry 3 bags.

   Steph Stretch can carry lots of bags.

   Steph Stretch can carry ☐ bags.

   How many more bags can Steph carry than Norma can?

Leap frogs

Unit 17/A

1. There are 58 frogs enjoying themselves in the water.

   Then 10 more frogs jump in the water.

   How many frogs are in the water now?

2. There are 37 frogs enjoying themselves sunbathing.

   Then 10 more frogs come to sunbathe.

   How many frogs are sunbathing now?

3. There are 10 frogs enjoying playing with a ball.

   Then 64 more frogs come to play with the ball.

   How many frogs are playing with the ball now?

Leap frogs

Unit 17/B

You fill in the missing numbers.

1. There are 25 frogs enjoying themselves in the water.

   ☐ more frogs jump in the water.

   How many frogs are in the water now?

2. There are 46 frogs enjoying themselves sunbathing.

   You decide how many more frogs come to sunbathe.

   ☐ more frogs come to sunbathe.

   How many frogs are sunbathing now?

3. There are 10 frogs enjoying playing with a ball.

   ☐ more frogs come to play with the ball.

   How many frogs are playing with the ball now?

Knock, knock

Unit 18/A

1. There are 40 people dancing on the disco floor.

   A bus arrives with 20 more people.

   How many people now dance?

2. There are 20 people watching the dancing.

   Then 40 more people sit down to watch the dancing.

   How many people now watch the dancing?

3. There are 30 people going to get food.

   Then 30 more people go to get some food.

   How many people are having food?

Knock, knock

Unit 18/B

Ask a friend to fill in the missing numbers.

1. There are 60 people dancing on the disco floor.

   A bus arrives with ☐ more people.

   How many people now dance?

2. There are 50 people watching the dancing.

   ☐ more people sit down to watch the dancing.

   How many people now watch the dancing?

3. There are 20 people going to get food.

   ☐ more people go to get some food.

   How many people are having food?

Sleeping Ugly

Unit 19/A

1. There are 62 ducks watching Drake dance.

   Then 10 ducks go off for tea.

   How many ducks stay to watch Drake dance?

2. There are 75 moorhens watching Serena dance.

   Then 10 moorhens go off for tea.

   How many moorhens stay to watch Serena dance?

3. There are 36 geese watching Drake and Serena dance.

   Then 10 more geese come to watch.

   How many geese are watching Drake and Serena dance?

Sleeping Ugly

Unit 19/B

You fill in the missing numbers.

1. There are 81 ducks watching Drake dance.

   ☐ ducks go off for tea.

   How many ducks stay to watch Drake dance?

2. There are 72 moorhens watching Serena dance.

   ☐ moorhens go off for tea.

   How many moorhens stay to watch Serena dance?

3. There are 18 geese watching Drake and Serena dance.

   ☐ more geese come to watch.

   How many geese are watching Drake and Serena dance?

Sam White

Unit 20/A

1. Sam White baked 80 cakes for the 7 giants.

   The 7 giants ate 50 cakes when they got home from work.

   How many cakes did they leave?

2. Sam White baked 90 biscuits for the 7 giants.

   The 7 giants ate 60 biscuits when they got home from work.

   How many biscuits did they leave?

3. Sam White baked 90 jam tarts for the 7 giants.

   The 7 giants ate 70 jam tarts when they got home from work.

   How many jam tarts did they leave?

Sam White

Unit 20/B

Ask a friend to fill in the missing numbers.

1. Sam White baked 90 cakes for the 7 giants.

   The 7 giants ate ☐ cakes, when they got home.

   How many cakes did they leave?

2. Sam White baked ☐ biscuits for the 7 giants.

   The 7 giants ate 20 biscuits when they got home.

   How many biscuits did they leave?

3. Sam White baked 50 jam tarts for the 7 giants.

   The 7 giants ate ☐ jam tarts when they got home.

   How many jam tarts did they leave?

BEAM's Big Book of Word Problems © BEAM Education

Rowdies

Unit 21/A

1. The Rowdies have 4 buckets.

   Each bucket has 5 slime sandwiches in it.

   How many slime sandwiches are there?

2. The Rowdies have 5 bowls.

   Each bowl has ten smelly jellies in it.

   How many smelly jellies are there?

3. Each box has 4 rotten apples in it.

   The Rowdies have 5 boxes.

   How many rotten apples are there?

Rowdies

Unit 21/B

You fill in the missing numbers.

1. The Rowdies have 6 buckets.

   Each bucket has ☐ slime sandwiches in it.

   How many slime sandwiches are there?

2. The Rowdies have ☐ bowls.

   Each bowl has ten smelly jellies in it.

   How many smelly jellies are there?

3. Each box has 5 rotten apples in it.

   The Rowdies have ☐ boxes.

   How many rotten apples are there?

Naughty Max

Unit 22/A

1. Max has chewed up some of Mike's stamps.

   How many stamps were there before Max chewed them?

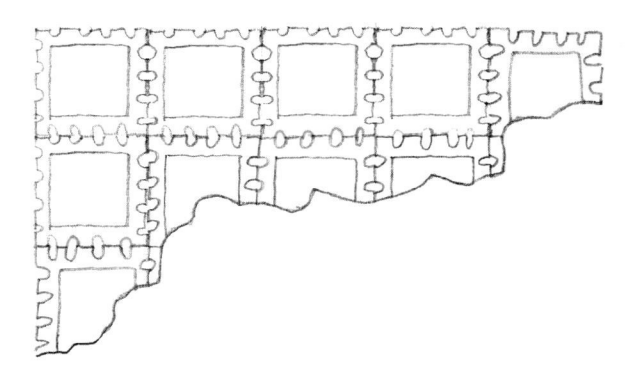

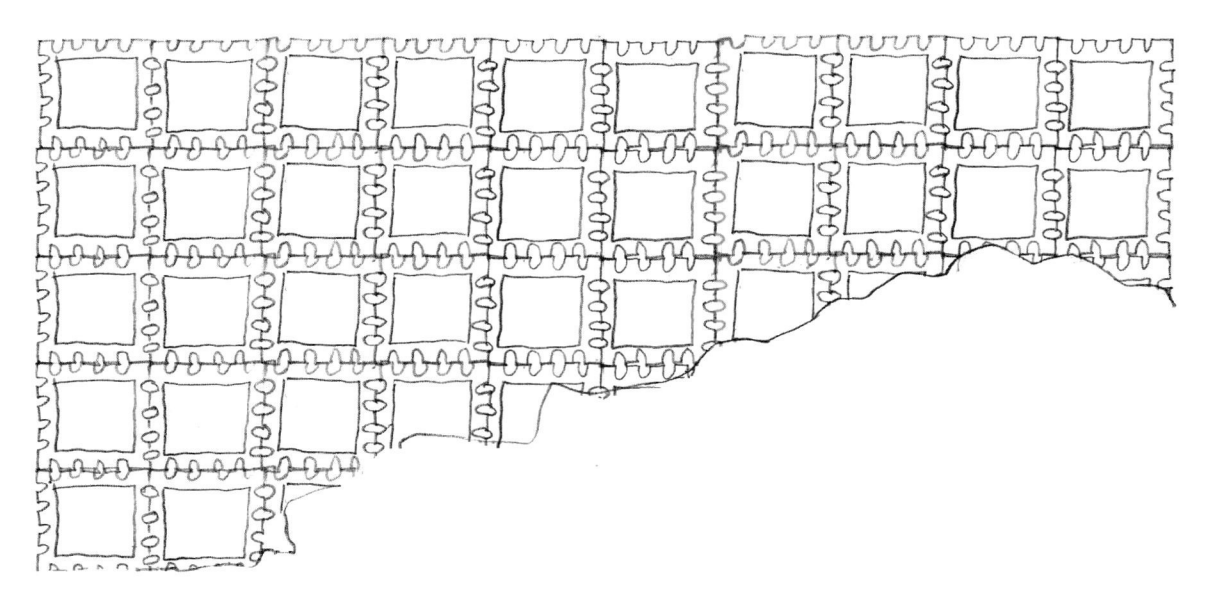

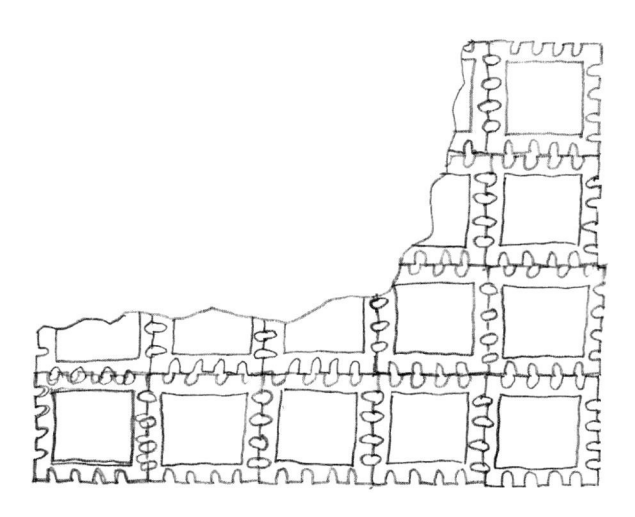

BEAM's Big Book of Word Problems © BEAM Education

Naughty Max

Unit 22/B

1. Tear a scrap of paper. Use it to hide some of the stamps.

   Ask your friend to work out how many stamps there are altogether.

   Now swap over.

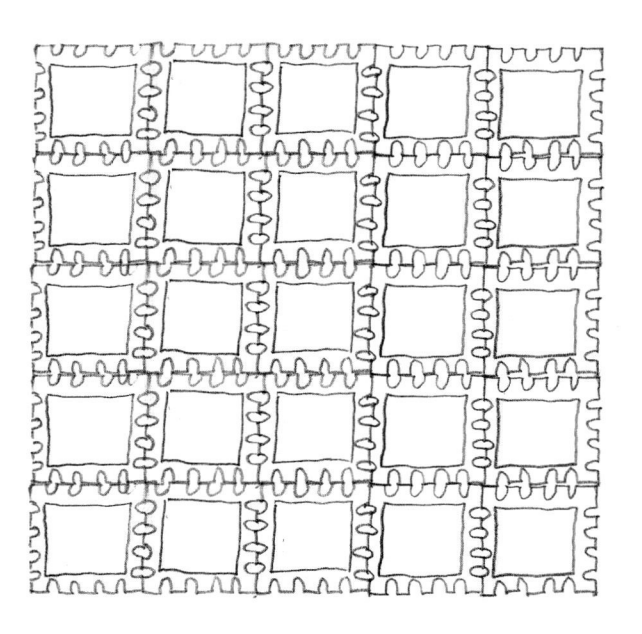

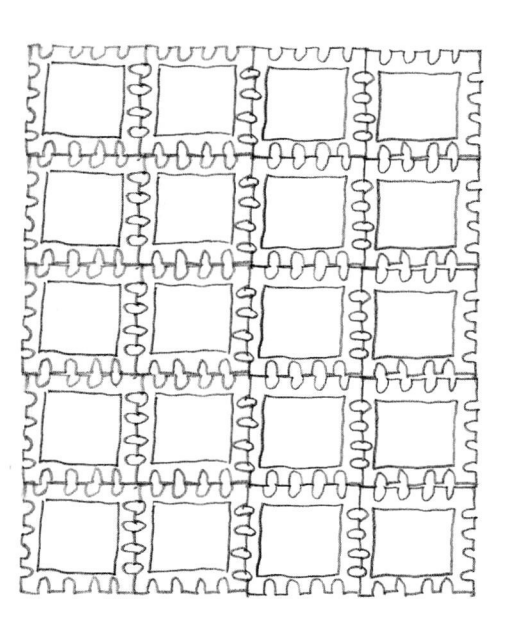

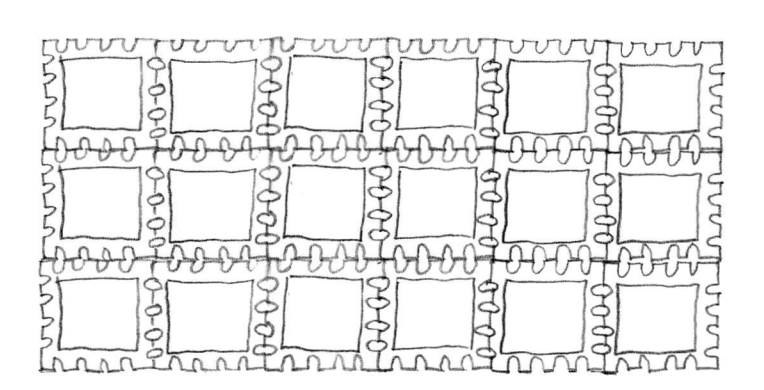

Mother and Father Goose   *Unit 23/A*

1. Mother Goose has 15 eggs.

   Mother Goose has 3 baskets.

   She puts the same number of eggs into each basket.

   How many eggs does Mother Goose put into each basket?

2. Father Goose has 4 boxes.

   Father Goose has 20 stones.

   He puts the same number of stones into each box.

   How many stones does Father Goose put into each box?

3. Baby Goose has 30 feathers.

   Baby Goose has 3 bags.

   She puts the same number of feathers into each bag.

   How many feathers does Baby Goose put into each bag?

Mother and Father Goose *Unit 23/B*

1. Mother Goose has 25 eggs.

   Mother Goose has 5 baskets.

   She puts the same number of eggs into each basket.

   How many eggs does Mother Goose put into each basket?

2. Father Goose has 12 stones.

   He puts the same number of stones into each box.

   Father Goose has 2 boxes. How many stones does Father Goose put into each box?

   Father Goose has 3 boxes. How many stones does Father Goose put into each box?

   Father Goose has 4 boxes. How many stones does Father Goose put into each box?

   Father Goose has 6 boxes. How many stones does Father Goose put into each box?

3. Baby Goose has 24 feathers.

   She wants to put the same number of feathers into each bag.

   Find some different ways of doing this.

Mary, Mary

Unit 24/A

1. Mary has 15 shells.

   She puts 5 shells in each bag.

   How many bags does Mary need for all her shells?

2. Mary puts 10 silver bells in each bag.

   Mary has 30 silver bells.

   How many bags does Mary need for all her silver bells?

3. Mary puts 3 sunflowers in each jar.

   Mary has 30 sunflowers.

   How many jars does Mary need for all her sunflowers?

Mary, Mary

Unit 24/B

1. Mary has 30 shells.

   She puts 6 shells in each bag.

   How many bags does Mary need for all her shells?

   One of her bags breaks, so Mary puts her 30 shells into 5 bags.

   How many shells does Mary put into each bag
   Each bag has the same number of shells.

2. Mary has 24 silver bells.

   Mary puts 2 silver bells into each bag.
   How many bags does Mary need for all her silver bells?

   Mary puts 3 silver bells into each bag.
   How many bags does Mary need for all her silver bells?

   Mary puts 4 silver bells into each bag.
   How many bags does Mary need for all her silver bells?

3. Mary has 36 sunflowers.

   Mary wants to put the same number of sunflowers into each jar.

   Find some ways that Mary can do this.

With thanks to the BEAM Development Group